The Magic & Mystery of

SPACE

Written by

Shoshana Z. Weider

DK

DK | Penguin Random House

Author Shoshana Z. Weider
Consultant Sophie Allan
Illustrator Claire McElfatrick
Editors John Hort, Lizzie Munsey
US Senior Editor Shannon Beatty
Designer Polly Appleton, Hannah Moore
Picture Researcher Rituraj Singh
Production Editor Gillian Reid
Production Controller Ben Radley
Managing Editor Penny Smith
Managing Art Editor Claire Patane
Art Director Mabel Chan
Publisher Francesca Young

First American Edition, 2025
Published in the United States by DK Publishing,
a division of Penguin Random House LLC
1745 Broadway, 20th Floor, New York, NY 10019

Published in Great Britain by Dorling Kindersley Limited

A catalog record for this book
is available from the Library of Congress.
ISBN 978-0-5939-5938-1

DK books are available at special discounts
when purchased in bulk for sales promotions,
premiums, fund-raising, or educational use.
For details, contact: DK Publishing Special Markets,
1745 Broadway, 20th Floor, New York, NY 10019
SpecialSales@dk.com

Printed and bound in China

www.dk.com

INTRODUCTION

Ever since I was young, there was nothing I found more awesome than gazing up at the night sky, or a full moon, and wondering about my place in the universe. I love that everyone can experience these same feelings by looking up to the stars, planets, and galaxies beyond our home.

So come with me to explore the magic that space holds. We will journey back to the beginning of time at the Big Bang, through our solar system, the places where we might find other life, and much, much more!

Shoshana Z. Weider

CONTENTS

Kármán line
The edge of space is often defined as being 62 miles (100 km) above sea level.

WHAT IS SPACE?

Space is enormous. It contains everything that has ever existed, including all the planets, stars, and galaxies.

It begins at the edge of Earth's atmosphere, where the air thins to almost nothing. This boundary is known as the Kármán line.

Space has fascinated people for centuries. Only a handful of people have ever ventured beyond the safety of Earth.

The universe

The planet we call home seems huge to us, but it is just a tiny dot in the vastness of the universe. The universe is everything there is, including space, and stretches out farther than we can imagine. It contains billions of stars, planets, rocks, and dust, but most of it is actually empty. So, how do we fit in?

Earth
We live on a planet called Earth. So far, it is the only place in the universe known to have life.

The solar system
Earth is one of eight planets in our solar system. At the center of the solar system is a star—the sun.

LIGHT YEARS

On Earth, we measure distances using miles or kilometers. In space, those measurements are so small they are almost useless. So, we measure space distances using light years. A light year is the distance light can travel in an Earth year. Each light year is around 6 trillion miles (10 trillion km).

Earth is approximately...

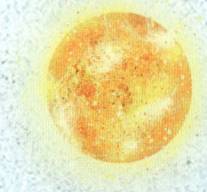

8.3 light minutes away from the sun, our closest star.

4.3 light years away from Proxima Centauri, our closest neighboring star.

26,000 light years away from the center of the Milky Way, our galaxy.

2.5 million light years away from Andromeda, the nearest large galaxy.

The universe
It is estimated that there are at least 200 billion galaxies in the universe!

The Milky Way
The sun is one of at least 100 billion stars that make up a galaxy called the Milky Way.

DARK, EMPTY NOTHINGNESS

Most of space appears dark, because there is nothing there to reflect light from the sun or other stars. Space has no air, so it is also completely silent, since sounds need air to be able to travel.

Light travels faster than anything else on Earth or in space.

Studying space

Humans started sending missions to space around 70 years ago, but ancient records show that people have been studying space for thousands of years. There are many ways to look into space without leaving Earth.

Telescopic views

Telescopes use lenses or mirrors to make things that are far away appear bigger. They were first used to study objects in space in the 1600s.

Keeping track

We can follow the movement of the sun, moon, and stars across the sky without using any special equipment. The earliest astronomers measured these movements, and used them to track time and create calendars.

Simple designs

The earliest telescopes were small and simply designed. You would look through one end and point the other at the object you wanted to see.

Lighting the way

Early telescopes could see only visible light, including the colors of the rainbow. However, modern telescopes can observe other types of light coming from stars and other objects in space.

Visible light

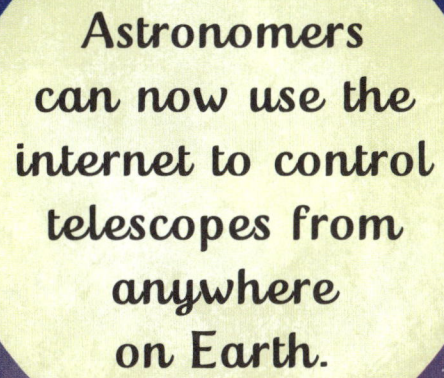

Astronomers can now use the internet to control telescopes from anywhere on Earth.

Big builds
The biggest telescopes are housed in big buildings, called observatories.

Exploded star

Jupiter in infrared light

Bigger and better
Today's telescopes that capture visible light can be more than 33 ft (10 m) long, which is longer than a bus. They are often built in deserts or on mountains, where there are few clouds to block their views.

Amazing space
Large telescopes give us amazing views of the universe, letting us learn more about space objects.

The Big Bang

Scientists think that the universe began suddenly, almost 14 billion years ago. It all started with an explosion from an unimaginably hot and dense single point, which contained all the material in the entire universe. The universe has been expanding and cooling ever since, and the galaxies are now millions of light years apart.

First second

5 minutes

380,000 years

Time begins
The expansion of the universe began within the first second after the explosion, or "Big Bang." At this stage, the universe was like an extremely hot "soup" of particles and light.

Early elements
During the next five minutes, the universe expanded and cooled enough for the atoms of the first chemical elements, such as hydrogen and helium, to form.

Oldest light
After 380,000 years, the universe was cool enough that tiny particles (electrons) were captured into atoms. Light could now travel across the universe.

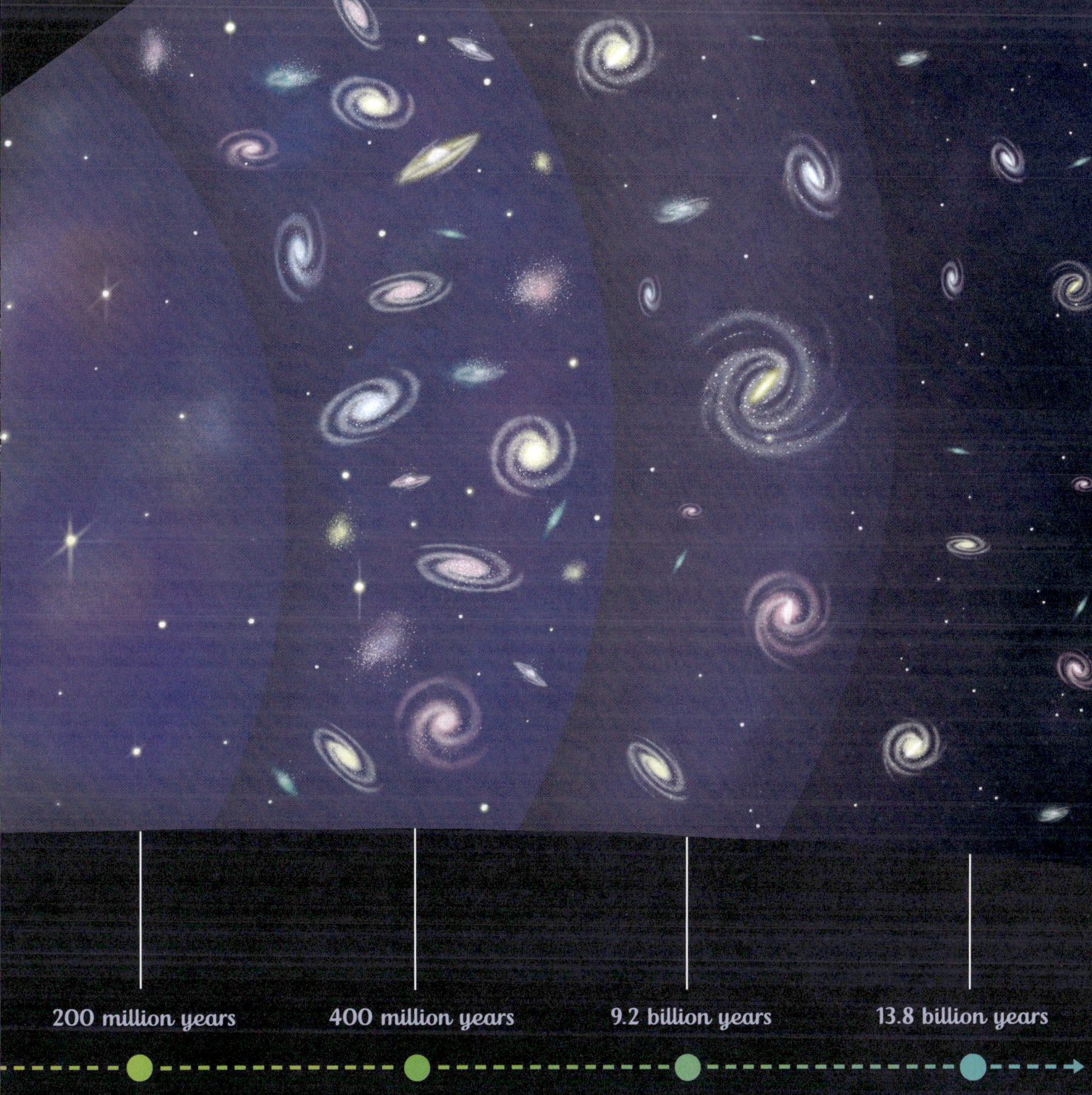

| 200 million years | 400 million years | 9.2 billion years | 13.8 billion years |

Early stars
Over the next hundreds of millions of years, lumpier areas pulled in more material. They got hotter and denser, forming huge, brightly shining stars.

First galaxies
After 400 million years, nearly all the hydrogen and helium had become stars. They grouped themselves into galaxies, which we can still see today.

Our solar system
Our sun formed about 4.6 billion years ago. The material around it came together, forming our solar system's planets.

The future
Astronomers believe that the universe is still expanding, and will continue to expand forever. This may be because of mysterious "dark energy."

OUR SOLAR SYSTEM

The solar system is everything that travels around our sun, held there by the sun's gravity. It includes the planets and their moons, asteroids, comets, and more!

Strong pull
The sun's gravitational pull is strong because it's so big.

The solar system is about 4.6 billion years old, but everything in it developed in different ways. This is why the planets, moons, asteroids, and other objects look different from one another. Scientists use clues from these objects today to help them understand the history of the solar system.

Everything around the sun

It's hard to say where the solar system ends. Its edge can be defined in many ways, such as by the reach of the sun's magnetic field, or where its gravity no longer dominates space. But we are certain that the sun's influence stretches for billions of miles. Scientists split the solar system into zones to help us understand it.

Level orbits

Most large objects in the solar system orbit (go around) the sun on the same horizontal level, which is known as the ecliptic plane. However, some objects, such as Pluto and some comets, orbit the sun on different planes.

Comet

Mars

Earth

Venus

Saturn

Kuiper belt

Pluto

There could be another **giant**

At the edge

The Oort cloud lies at the solar system's edge. It contains billions of icy and rocky bodies, and may be where many comets come from. It stretches almost halfway to the next star!

Oort cloud

Uranus

Main asteroid belt

Jupiter

Outer solar system

Comet

Inner Solar System

Sun

Mercury

Comet

Neptune

planet far beyond Neptune, but we haven't found it yet.

Solar flares
High-energy bursts of radiation from the sun's surface are known as solar flares.

Solar cycle

The sun's energy is not constant—it changes throughout an 11-year cycle. It is most active at "solar maximum." This is when there are the most sunspots and solar flares.

The sun

The sun is an extremely hot ball of gas, with temperatures reaching millions of degrees. It is mostly made of hydrogen and helium. The sun's size and temperature are pretty average compared with other stars, but it is special—its heat provides the energy that supports almost all life on Earth.

Core

Radiative zone

Convection zone

Chromosphere

Solar flare

Sunspot

Corona

Solar wind

INSIDE THE SUN

Each layer of the sun has a different temperature. The core is the hottest, reaching up to 27 million°F (15 million°C).

SOLAR ECLIPSES

Total solar eclipses happen when the moon perfectly blocks light from the sun. During these rare events, only the sun's corona (outer atmosphere) is visible.

Big future
In 5 billion years, the sun will become a red giant. It will be at least 100 times larger.

Water world
Earth's surface is 71 percent water.

Middling size
Earth is the fifth-largest planet in the solar system.

We can't journey inside Earth, but geologists can use earthquake waves to study its layers.

Earth

Earth is a terrestrial, or "rocky," planet. It is unique within the solar system because it has oceans of liquid water on its surface. We use our understanding of Earth to help us learn about the other planets.

INSIDE EARTH

Earth is made up of four layers: the crust, mantle, outer core, and inner core. It also has a layer of gases around it, which is called the atmosphere.

Crust
The top layer of Earth is the crust. It is made of solid rock, which can change over time as it is worn away by wind and water, or pushed around by tectonics. This is the part of Earth that we can see.

Mantle
Earth's mantle is also made of rocky material. When it melts, it can rise up to Earth's surface and form new rocks.

Atmosphere
Earth's atmosphere is made of a mixture of gases—mostly nitrogen and oxygen. Almost all of our weather happens in the lowest part of the atmosphere, which is called the troposphere.

Outer core
The outer part of the core is made of liquid metal. It moves around in currents, like water draining from a bath. This movement helps create Earth's magnetic field.

Inner core
The inner core is a solid ball of metal: mostly iron and nickel. Its temperature is almost 9,932°F (5,500°C), which is as hot as the surface of the sun.

Pale blue dot

The most distant photo of Earth was taken by the Voyager 1 spacecraft, from 3.8 billion miles (6.1 billion km) away.

Earth

The moon

The moon is Earth's only natural satellite (something that orbits a planet) and our closest neighbor in space. The oldest rocks on the moon's surface are almost as old as the solar system—much older than the oldest parts of Earth.

THE MOON'S FACE

We can only see one side of the moon from Earth, which we call the near side. The light and dark areas we see are made of different types of rocks.

Mare
The black areas are made of a rock called basalt. Early astronomers thought they were bodies of water, and named them "mare," which is the Latin word for "sea."

Highlands
The white areas are made of a rock called anorthosite and have mountains.

Tycho
All of the craters on the moon are named after scientists. Tycho is one of the brightest and most visible craters.

IMPACT CRATERS

The moon has no atmosphere to protect it, so its surface is pitted with craters. These form when space rocks smash into the moon. The moon's biggest crater is 1,500 miles (2,500 km) wide, but most are much smaller.

GIANT IMPACT

Scientists believe the moon formed almost 4.5 billion years ago, after a massive collision between the early Earth and another early planet, Theia. The dust and rock from that collision became the moon.

Theia

Moon

Earth

TWO PLANETS
When Earth first formed, it didn't have a moon.

IMPACT
Theia collided with Earth, and smashed itself into pieces.

DEBRIS RING
The debris from the impact formed a ring around Earth.

NEW MOON
Over time, the debris came together to form the moon.

MOON ROCKS

The rocks on the moon's surface are mostly shades of white, gray, and black. But in some areas, there are also colorful glass beads that formed during volcanic eruptions. Moon rocks can be retrieved by missions, but sometimes the rocks come to us as meteorites!

METEORITE
This gray-colored moon rock is a lunar meteorite: it fell to Earth after being knocked into space by an impact on the moon's surface.

APOLLO 11
This dark-colored rock was brought back to Earth by astronauts on the first mission to the moon, Apollo 11.

GIFT ROCK
This basalt was brought back by the Apollo 17 mission. Fragments of it were given to countries around the world.

GLASS
These glass beads formed billions of years ago. Various missions have brought "moon glass" back to Earth.

Mercury's surface is gray. The colors here tell us about the different types of rock.

Caloris Basin
This is Mercury's largest impact crater.

Orange areas
These show where there are volcanic rocks, which formed from liquid lava.

Light-blue areas
These show young impact craters and the material that was thrown out from them.

Dark-blue areas
These are the oldest rocks on Mercury's surface.

Mercury

Mercury is a planet of extremes. It is the closest planet to the sun and the smallest in the solar system. It has no atmosphere to hold in heat. So, the surface temperature plunges from a searingly hot 806°F (430°C) in the day to a freezing cold –292°F (–180°C) at night.

Shrinking planet
Mercury has many long, curved cliffs. They formed because Mercury is slowly shriveling up. It has shrunk by about 4.3 miles (7 km) since it formed, billions of years ago.

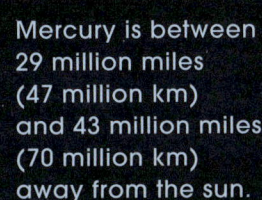

Mercury is between 29 million miles (47 million km) and 43 million miles (70 million km) away from the sun.

Days and years

One year on Mercury is equal to 88 Earth days. However, the planet spins so slowly that it only rotates three times for every two trips around the sun, meaning there are three Mercury days for every two Mercury years.

Massive core

Like Earth, Mercury has a mantle and core beneath its crust. Mercury's core is huge—it makes up more than half of the planet. Mercury also has a magnetic field, which tells us that the outer part of its core is made of liquid metal.

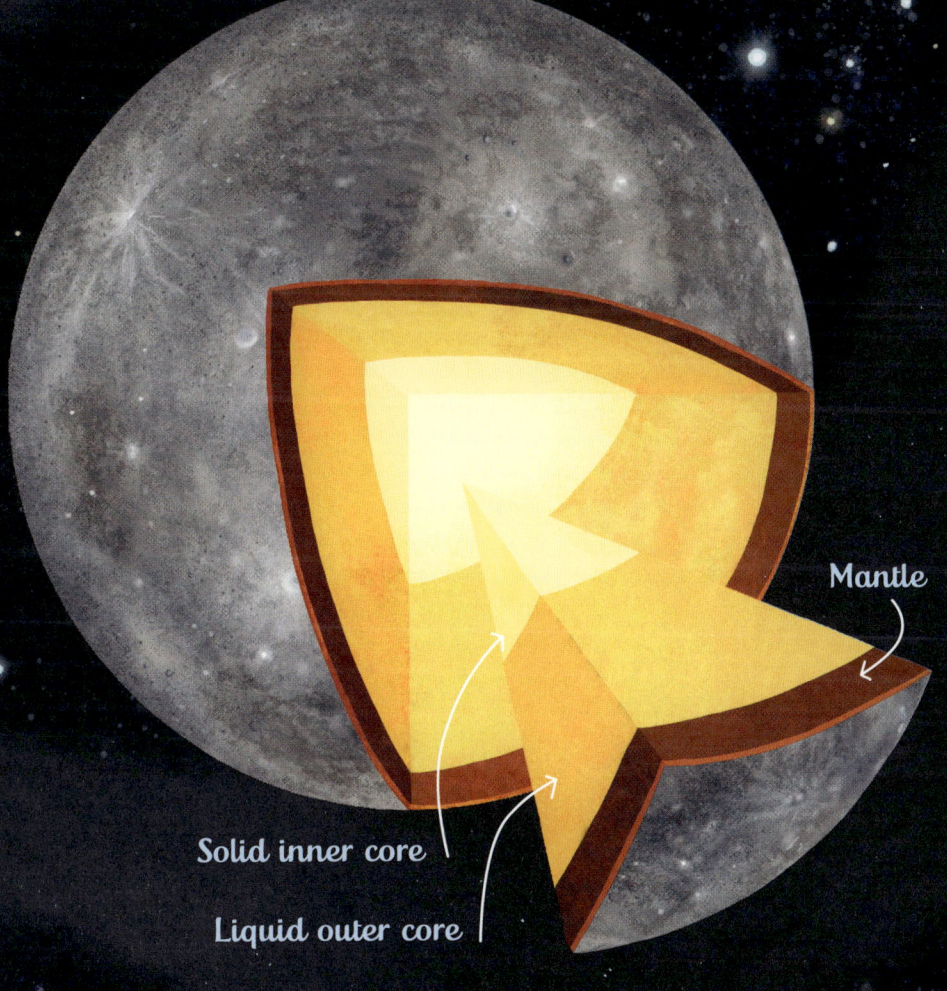

Mantle

Solid inner core

Liquid outer core

Polar ice

Craters near Mercury's north and south poles have areas that are never directly lit by the sun. These permanently shadowed regions are some of the coldest places in the entire solar system. Scientists think they contain ice, which was carried there by comets.

Sunlight

Permanent shadow

Water-carrying comet

Ice left behind

POISONOUS ATMOSPHERE

Venus' atmosphere is extremely thick. It is made mostly of carbon dioxide—a gas that is poisonous to humans. This dense atmosphere traps heat around the planet, which makes Venus the hottest planet in the whole solar system.

Venus is covered with a thick layer of sulphuric acid clouds, which makes it impossible to see the surface with our eyes or standard cameras. Spacecraft use special radar instruments to observe the planet's surface.

Venus

Venus is a similar size to Earth, and the two planets are fairly close to each other. Billions of years ago they may have been very similar, but they have changed in different ways over time. Today, Venus is extremely hot and inhospitable—it is often described as Earth's evil twin.

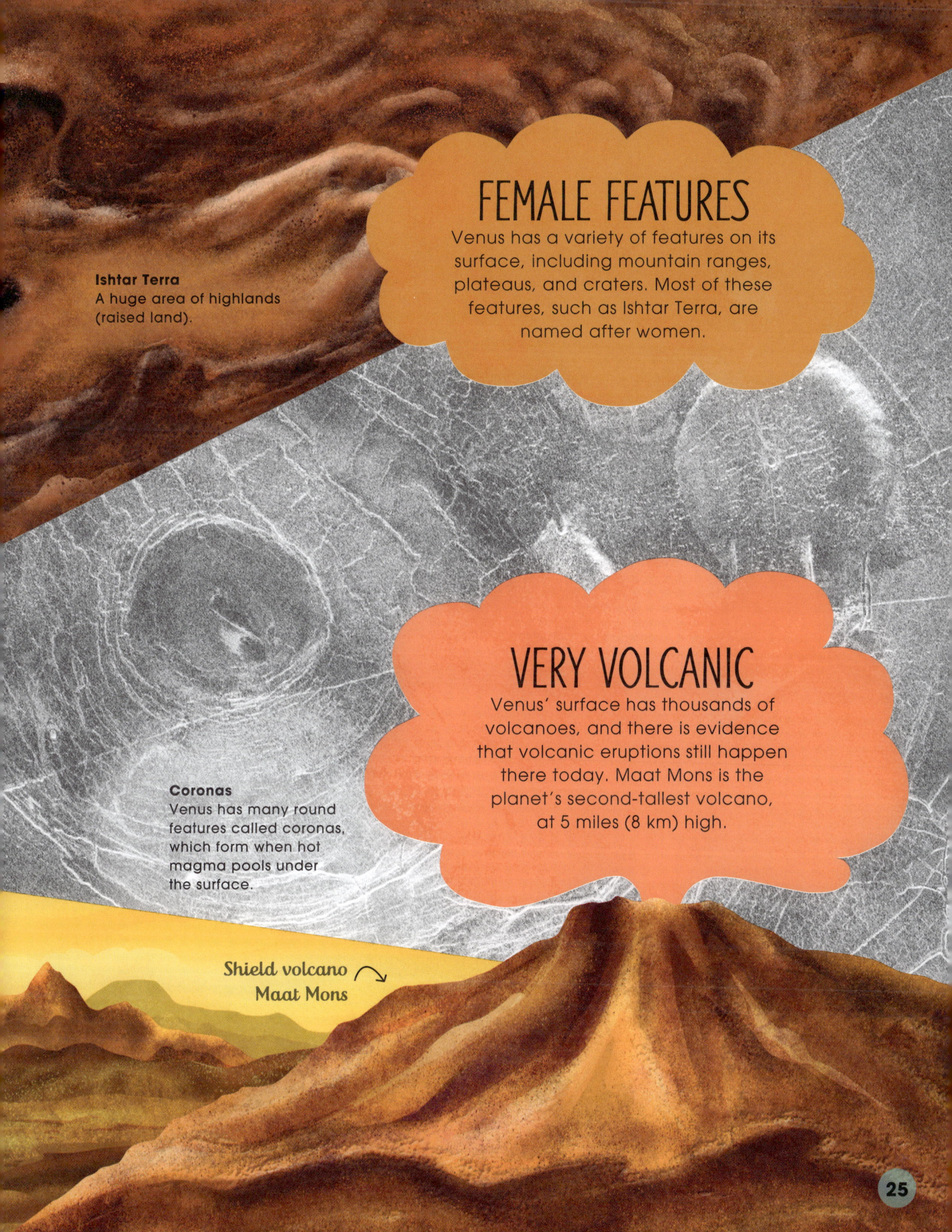

Ishtar Terra
A huge area of highlands (raised land).

FEMALE FEATURES

Venus has a variety of features on its surface, including mountain ranges, plateaus, and craters. Most of these features, such as Ishtar Terra, are named after women.

Coronas
Venus has many round features called coronas, which form when hot magma pools under the surface.

VERY VOLCANIC

Venus' surface has thousands of volcanoes, and there is evidence that volcanic eruptions still happen there today. Maat Mons is the planet's second-tallest volcano, at 5 miles (8 km) high.

Shield volcano
Maat Mons

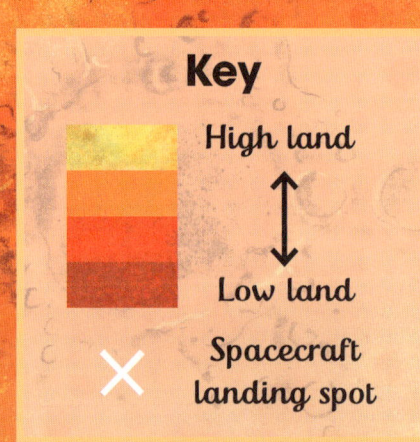

Giant volcano

Mars has many volcanoes. The most impressive is Olympus Mons, the biggest volcano in the solar system. It is 388 miles (625 km) wide and three times taller than Earth's Mount Everest!

✕ Phoenix lander

Ingenuity was a NASA-designed robot helicopter, which flew on Mars between 2021 and 2024.

Olympus Mons

Viking lander ✕

✕
Pathfinder rover

Valles Marineris

Massive valley

Valles Marineris is a huge valley near Mars' equator. It is about ten times longer than Earth's Grand Canyon. Valles Marineris probably formed when part of Mars' crust cracked open.

Key

High land

Low land

✕ Spacecraft landing spot

Mars

Mars is known as the Red Planet, because it is covered in a reddish-colored dust. The red color is caused by rusting iron in the minerals on Mars' surface. Humans have been fascinated with Mars for centuries, and many kinds of robotic spacecraft have been sent to explore it.

Viking 2 lander
✕

Try, try, try again

Since the 1960s, around 50 spacecraft have been sent to expore Mars. Many of them failed, but scientists have so many important questions about Mars that new missions keep being sent there. Some are marked on this map.

✕
Perseverance rover

InSight lander
✕

Opportunity rover
✕

Curiosity rover
✕

Spirit rover
✕

Twin moons

Mars has two small moons called Phobos and Deimos, which look a little like potatoes. Scientists are still studying how these moons formed. Some people think they were asteroids that were captured by Mars' gravity.

Phobos

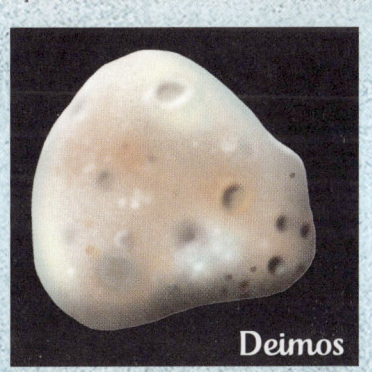
Deimos

Asteroids and meteorites

Asteroids are large, rocky objects that orbit the sun as leftovers from the birth of the solar system. When chunks of asteroids break off and travel through Earth's atmosphere to hit the ground they are known as meteorites.

ASTEROID
There are more than 1 million asteroids in the solar system. They come in a range of sizes.

Most meteorites come from asteroids or protoplanets, but some are from the moon and Mars.

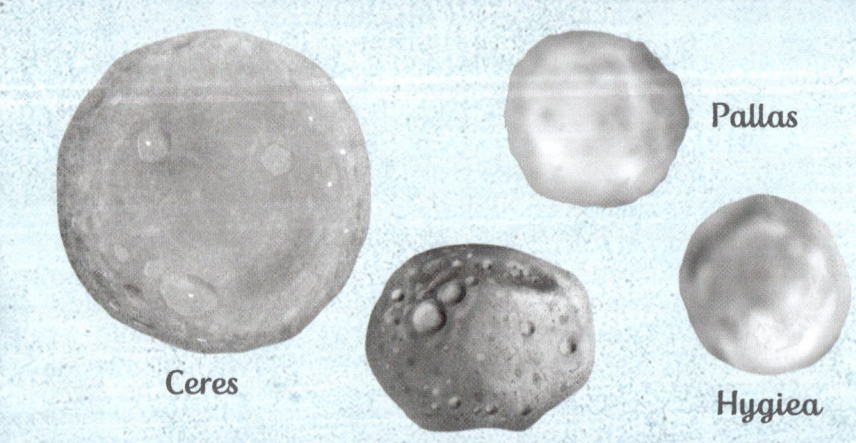

Ceres

Pallas

Vesta

Hygiea

Asteroid belt
Most asteroids orbit the sun in an area between Mars and Jupiter, which is known as the asteroid belt. The four biggest bodies here are called Ceres, Vesta, Pallas, and Hygiea.

METEOROID

Meteoroids are small lumps of rock that orbit the sun. They are usually pebble-sized.

METEOR SHOWER

When many meteors appear in one part of the sky at a particular time of year it is known as a meteor shower. They happen because Earth is moving through lots of debris in space.

METEOR

Once meteoroids enter Earth's atmosphere they are known as meteors, or shooting stars. The light we see is the rock burning up in Earth's atmosphere.

Iron meteorite

Stony meteorite

FIREBALL

Large meteors create very bright fireballs in the sky as they burn up. Some parts of the rock may survive to reach the ground.

METEORITE

Meteorites are divided into types based on the materials they are made of. These materials tell us about the place they originally came from.

Earth's atmosphere

Stony-iron meteorite

Giant planets

The outer four planets in the solar system are much bigger than the inner four. They formed farther from the sun, where it is much colder. These giant planets have dense cores surrounded by huge amounts of gas, with no solid surfaces.

Other planets have rings, but Saturn's are the most famous. They are made from chunks of ice, rock, and dust, and each ring orbits Saturn at a different speed.

Hexagonal storm

Rings

Jupiter's stripes are bands of clouds, formed by swirling winds. The Great Red Spot is a huge and long-lived storm, which is about the size of Earth.

Jupiter's moon, Io

The Great Red Spot

JUPITER

Jupiter is the largest planet in the solar system: it is double the size of all the other planets put together. It is made mostly of hydrogen and helium, and has almost 100 moons, including Io.

SATURN

Saturn has a mysterious, giant, hexagon-shaped storm at its north pole. It also has the most moons of all the planets. Saturn's largest moon, Titan, has lakes made of methane.

Uranus' solid core

Scientists think that Uranus has a solid core, an icy mantle, and a hydrogen- and helium-rich, gassy atmosphere.

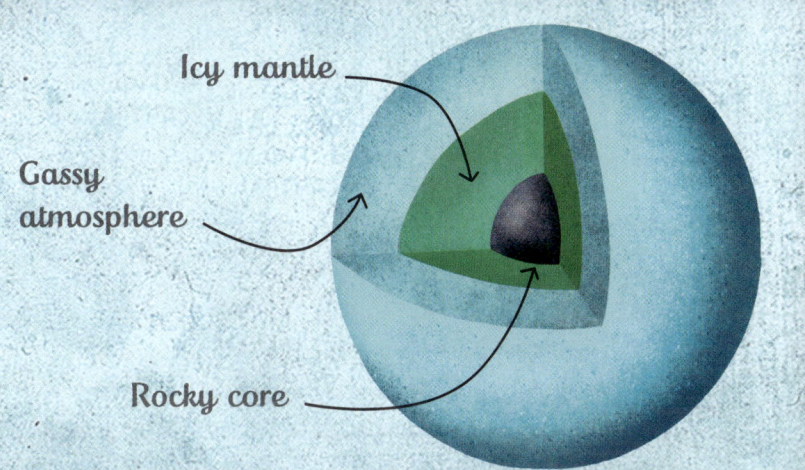

Icy mantle

Gassy atmosphere

Rocky core

Uranus may have been knocked onto its side in a long-ago collision.

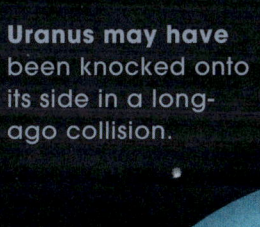

Pole

Neptune's atmosphere contains methane, which absorbs the red part of light. This is what makes the planet appear blue to us.

Clouds of methane

URANUS

Uranus is unusual because it orbits the sun on its side: its pole is horizontal rather than upright. It also turns on its axis in the opposite direction compared with most of the planets.

NEPTUNE

The farthest planet from the sun, Neptune has an orbit that lasts 165 Earth years. It is the only planet not visible with the naked eye, and only one spacecraft has visited it—Voyager 2, in 1989.

Outer solar system

In the outer solar system, beyond Neptune, lies the Kuiper belt. This ring is about 1.8 billion miles (3 billion km) wide. It is made up of billions of small, icy bodies that were left over from the birth of the solar system.

Sun

ICY BODIES

Many of the icy bodies in the Kuiper belt are small, but some are large enough to be classed as dwarf planets. The largest body that we know of in the Kuiper belt is the dwarf planet Pluto. Pluto has a number of moons, including Charon.

Charon

Pluto

Arrokoth

New Horizons
spacecraft

New Horizons

NASA's New Horizons spacecraft is journeying through the Kuiper belt. It visited Pluto in 2015, and took images of another Kuiper belt object, Arrokoth, in 2019. Arrokoth is made of two smaller objects joined together, and looks a bit like a snowman.

Comets travel from the edge of our solar system.

COMETS

Comets are small balls of ice and rock, which journey from the outer solar system and around the sun in oval-shaped orbits. As a comet approaches the sun, its ice warms up and evaporates, creating a long tail behind it, called a coma.

Comet orbits

Comets take different amounts of time to orbit the sun. Halley's Comet makes the journey about once every 75 years.

Halley's
Comet

Two tails
A comet has a gas tail and a dust tail, both of which always point away from the sun. They get longer when the comet travels close to the sun.

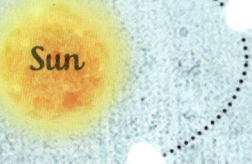

Sun

Gas tail

Dust tail

This NASA James Webb Space Telescope image shows thousands of galaxies, billions of light years away from Earth.

BEYOND THE SOLAR SYSTEM

Our solar system is just a tiny part of the universe. Beyond it lies the vastness of "deep space," which contains huge numbers of stars, galaxies, and other space objects.

Our sun is just one star of around 100 billion that make up the Milky Way Galaxy. Experts think the universe contains somewhere between 200 billion and two trillion galaxies—a number so big that it is almost impossible to imagine.

Nebulas

These colossal clouds of swirling gas and dust exist in interstellar space—in the spaces between the stars. Nebulas are the places where new stars and planets are born. They can also be left behind by dying stars.

The "Pillars of Creation" in the Eagle Nebula is an area where new stars are still forming.

The Pillars of Creation

Birth of the sun

Our solar system formed from a nebula, called the Solar Nebula. This nebula was created by the explosion of an earlier star in the Milky Way. This means our sun is a second- or third-generation star.

Bright Orion

The Orion Nebula is the brightest nebula in the night sky, and one of only a few that can be seen with the naked eye. It is positioned in the constellation Orion.

INCREDIBLE VIEWS

Nebulas come in a range of shapes and sizes. They can be very beautiful, as is shown by these telescopic images.

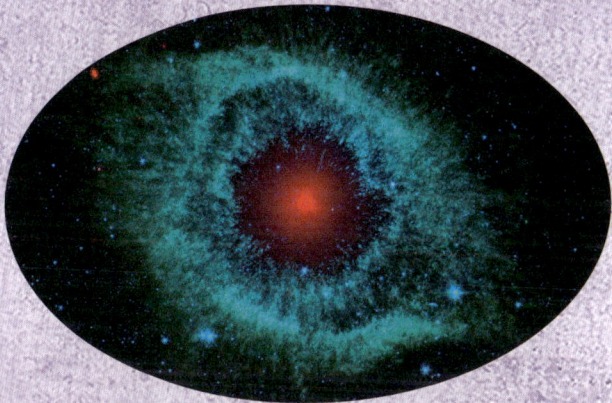

The Helix Nebula is 650 million light years away—one of the closest nebulas to Earth. It can be found in the constellation Aquarius.

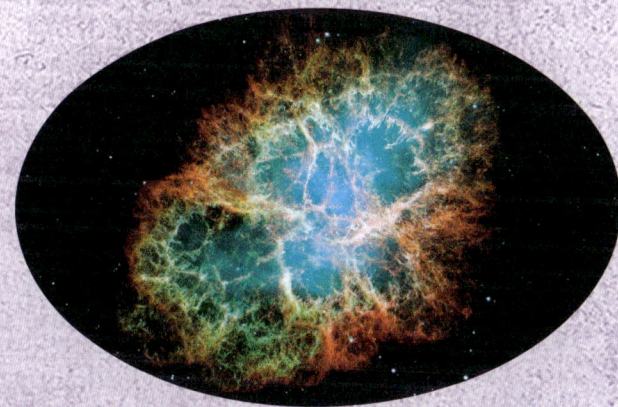

The Crab Nebula is a cloud that was left behind after a star exploded in 1054. The explosion was observed by Chinese astronomers.

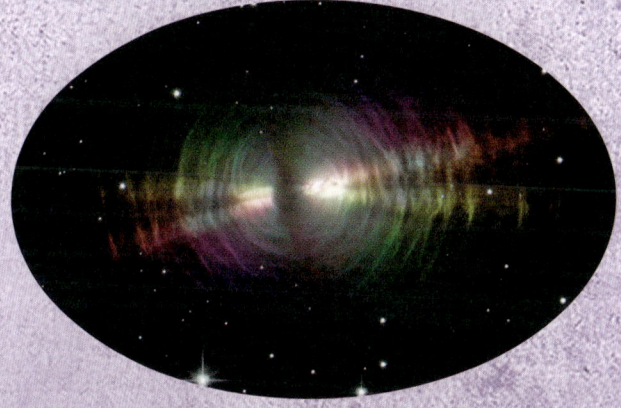

The Egg Nebula has a series of bright circles around a central star, which is hidden by thick clouds.

Bellatrix

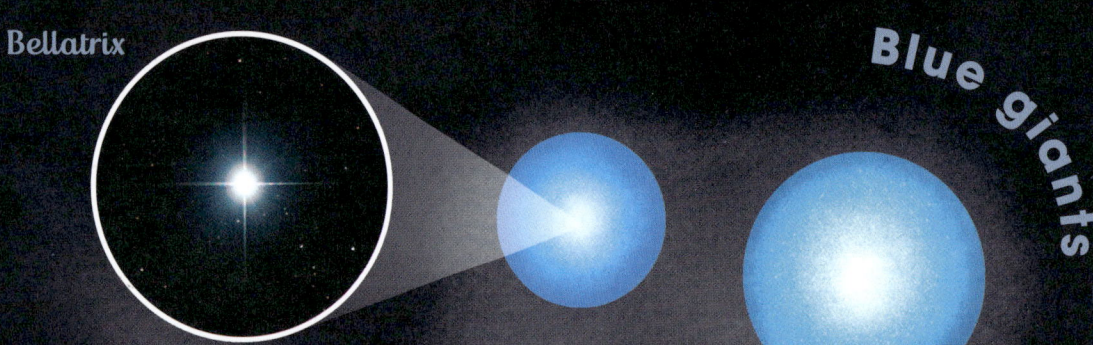

Blue giants

Blue giants are large, very hot stars, which are relatively rare.

White dwarfs are the leftover cores of red giants. They are about the size of Earth, but much heavier, and are gradually cooling down.

Sirius B

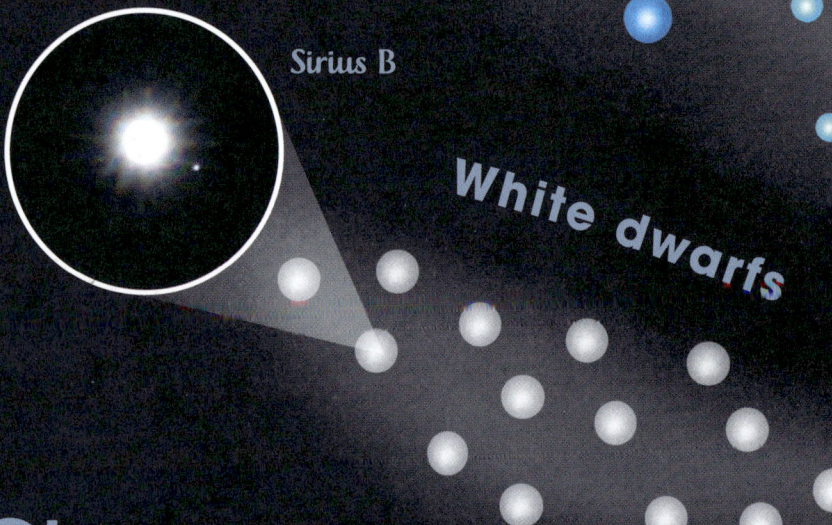

White dwarfs

Stars

Stars are extremely hot balls of glowing gas, which astronomers have been studying for centuries. They have learned enough about stars that we are able to group them, based on their size, temperature, and brightness. Individual stars move between groups during their life cycles.

VERY HOT

UY Scuti is one of the largest stars— 5 billion suns could fit inside it!

Red giants are stars that have run out of hydrogen to burn in their cores. Without hydrogen the star expands, cools, and throws off its atmosphere.

Red giants

Supergiants

Supergiants are the biggest, heaviest, and brightest stars. They are at least ten times heavier than the sun, and can be a thousand times larger.

Betelgeuse

Arcturus

Pretty ordinary

Compared with other stars, the sun is very average. It is known as a main sequence star: in the middle in terms of its size, temperature, and brightness.

Sun

Sun

Main sequence

About 90 percent of stars are in the main sequence, where they can live for millions or billions of years.

Stellar company

Many stars are actually part of systems where multiple stars orbit each other. The nearest star to Earth is Proxima Centauri. It is part of a triple star system, with Rigil Kentaurus and Toliman.

HOT   COOL

Life cycle of a star

Stars do not stay the same throughout their long lives: they change size, color, and temperature. Most stars live for a million or a few billion years, but some can live even longer. The way stars eventually die depends on how big they are, which we call their mass.

Smaller stars follow this path.

Our sun is currently in its middle age.

Larger stars follow this path.

STAR BIRTH

The first stage in a star's life is when a protostar forms inside a cloud of gas and dust called a nebula. Protostars spin very quickly and can last for thousands of years.

MIDDLE AGE

In its middle age, a "main sequence" star fuses hydrogen atoms into helium in its core. How long it spends in this stage depends on its size—the bigger the star, the quicker its hydrogen is used up.

Black holes are extremely hard to detect—the first image of one was only taken in 2019.

Nebulas form amazing patterns of dust and gas.

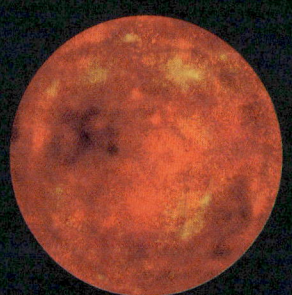

White dwarfs are very dense.

RED GIANT

Once the hydrogen in the core of a smaller star is gone, the star collapses. The hydrogen in the star's atmosphere now burns, and the star's outer layers expand and cool.

NEBULA

When all the star's fuel has been consumed, its outer layers are thrown out into space. This creates a nebula of dust and gas around a tiny core made mostly of carbon and oxygen.

WHITE DWARF

The remaining core is a white dwarf, which starts off extremely hot and glowing white. Eventually, white dwarfs will cool down and become black dwarfs, but the universe isn't old enough for these yet.

These are the largest known stars.

NEUTRON STAR

What remains after a supernova depends on the mass of the star's core. Smaller cores become neutron stars, the densest stars in the universe.

SUPERNOVA

A supergiant reaches the end of its life in a spectacular explosion called a supernova. It shrinks very fast, and its temperature reaches billions of degrees. Supernovas are some of the brightest events in the universe.

BLACK HOLE

Stars with larger cores become black holes after a supernova. Their gravity is so strong that the star collapses into a single, extremely dense point.

RED SUPERGIANT

Once the hydrogen in a larger star runs out, it begins to fuse other elements instead. A star at this stage is huge—if the sun were a supergiant, it would reach Jupiter!

Galaxies

Galaxies are groups of stars, planets, and clouds of rock, gas, and dust held together by gravity. The smallest have thousands of stars and are a few hundred light years wide. The largest galaxies—supergiants—contain trillions of stars and are millions of light years across. Galaxies can be organized into categories based on their shapes.

NGC 612
This lenticular galaxy
is 388 million light
years away.

SPIRAL

Spiral galaxies look like swirling pinwheels. They are flat disks with a central bulge and lots of stars. The spiral arms extend from the bulge and are where the youngest stars form.

LENTICULAR

Lenticular means "lens-shaped." Lenticular galaxies have central bulges, but without any arms around them. The stars in lenticular galaxies are mostly older, with few new ones being born.

Messier 82
This irregular galaxy is 12 million light years away.

"NGC" stands for "New General Catalog"—a list of 7,840 interesting things in the night sky, which each have their own number.

NGC 4150
This galaxy is around 45 million light years away.

IRREGULAR

Irregular galaxies come in a range of strange shapes, and contain a mixture of old and young stars. The force of gravity from neighboring galaxies may be what pulls irregular galaxies into unusual shapes.

ELLIPTICAL

Elliptical galaxies appear smooth and round. They range from completely circular to more oval-shaped. Scientists think elliptical galaxies may form when older galaxies collide and merge together.

Not alone

The Milky Way is one of about 50 galaxies in a cluster called the Local Group. The nearest galaxy to us is the Andromeda Galaxy. The Milky Way is the second largest of the local group—smaller than the Andromeda, but larger than the next biggest galaxy, called the Triangulum.

THE LOCAL GROUP

Andromeda Galaxy

Triangulum Galaxy

Milky Way Galaxy

The Milky Way

Our galaxy, the Milky Way, is a barred spiral shape: its stars spiral outward from a bar-shaped central bulge. The sun and our solar system sit in one of the outer spirals, known as the Orion-Cygnus Arm, which is about 27,000 light years from the center. Astronomers believe the Milky Way is more than 13 billion years old.

We got the name the "Milky Way" from the ancient Romans, who called it "the road of milk" because it looks like a hazy belt across the night sky.

Central bulge

Our solar system

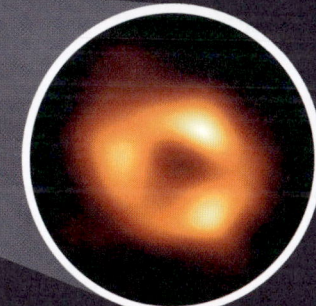

At the center

Astronomers believe there is a massive black hole at the center of the Milky Way, called Sagittarius A. Everything else in the galaxy rotates around this central black hole.

Exoplanets

The first planet orbiting a star other than the sun was discovered in 1992. We call these extra-solar planets "exoplanets." Since 1992, scientists have discovered more than 5,000 of them. Astronomers use several techniques to detect these distant worlds. Taking direct images of them is actually one of the harder ways to find them.

Scientists estimate that there could be up to a trillion exoplanets in our galaxy alone.

A world of worlds

Exoplanets come in a wide range of sizes, and orbit their stars at many different distances. We divide them into four different categories:

GAS GIANTS

These gassy exoplanets are huge, like Jupiter, and some are even bigger.

EARTHLIKE PLANETS

About 40 light years away is a set of seven rocky exoplanets known as the TRAPPIST-1 system. These exoplanets are very interesting to scientists because they are about the same size as Earth, and may have water on their surfaces. This means that they are promising places to look for extraterrestrial life.

TRAPPIST-1 system

Planet B is 1.09 times the width of Earth.

Planet C is 1.06 times the width of Earth.

Less light: more planets

Most exoplanets have been found using the "transit method." When a planet moves in front of its star, the amount of light detected by telescopes drops very slightly, showing us that a planet is there.

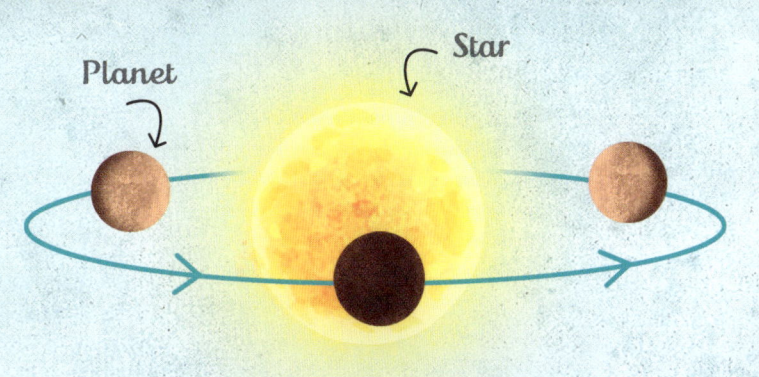

Planet

Star

NEPTUNE-LIKE

These exoplanets are similar in size to Neptune or Uranus. They have gassy atmospheres.

SUPER-EARTH

These are rocky planets larger than Earth, but smaller than Neptune.

TERRESTRIAL

Earth-sized or smaller, these exoplanets are made from rock and metal.

Planet D is 0.77 times the width of Earth.

Planet E is 0.92 times the width of Earth.

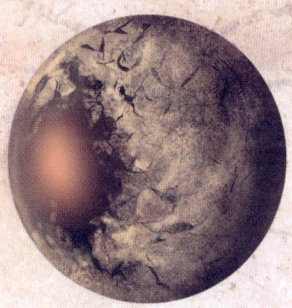

Planet F is 1.04 times the width of Earth.

Planet G is 1.13 times the width of Earth.

Planet H is 0.76 times the width of Earth.

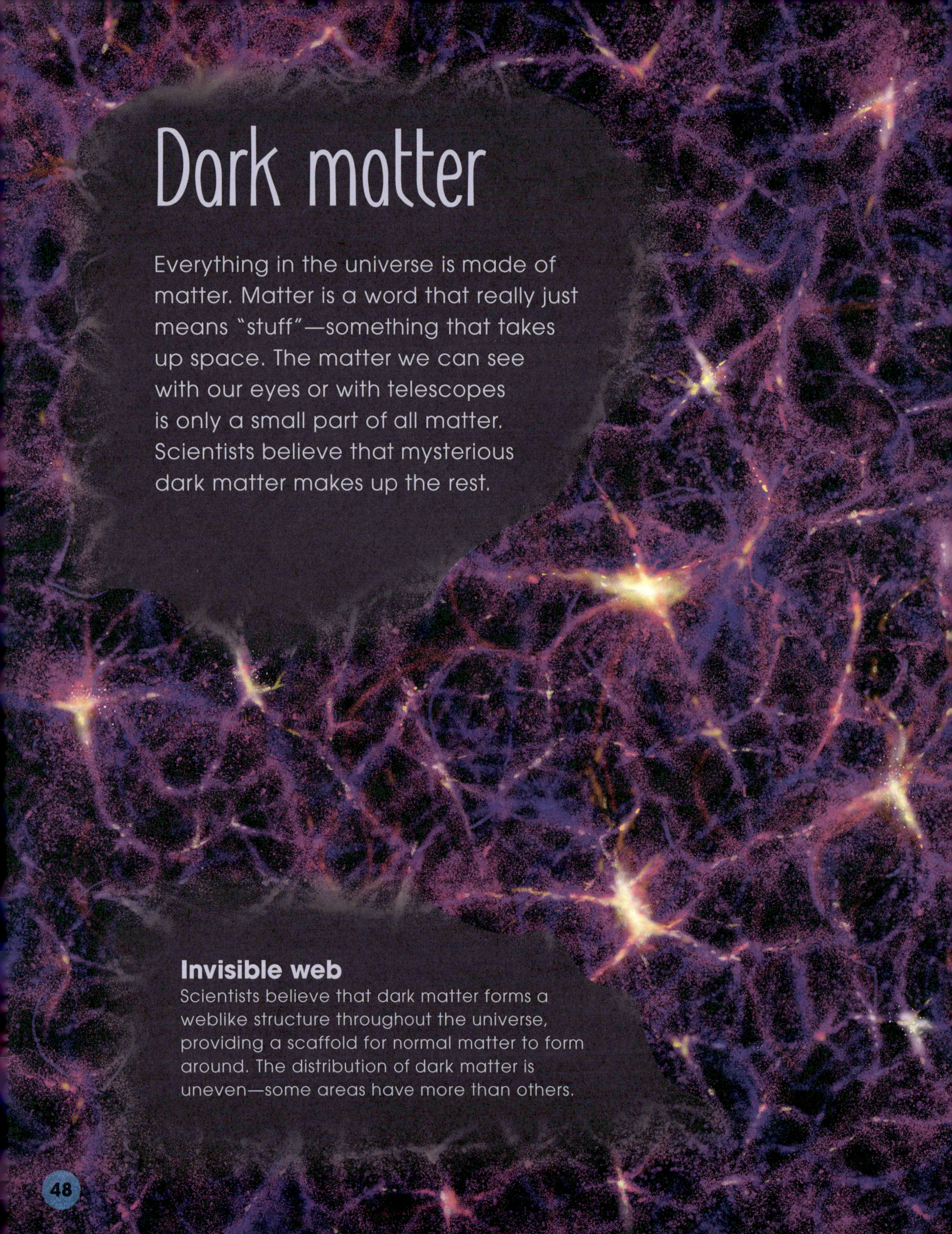

Dark matter

Everything in the universe is made of matter. Matter is a word that really just means "stuff"—something that takes up space. The matter we can see with our eyes or with telescopes is only a small part of all matter. Scientists believe that mysterious dark matter makes up the rest.

Invisible web

Scientists believe that dark matter forms a weblike structure throughout the universe, providing a scaffold for normal matter to form around. The distribution of dark matter is uneven—some areas have more than others.

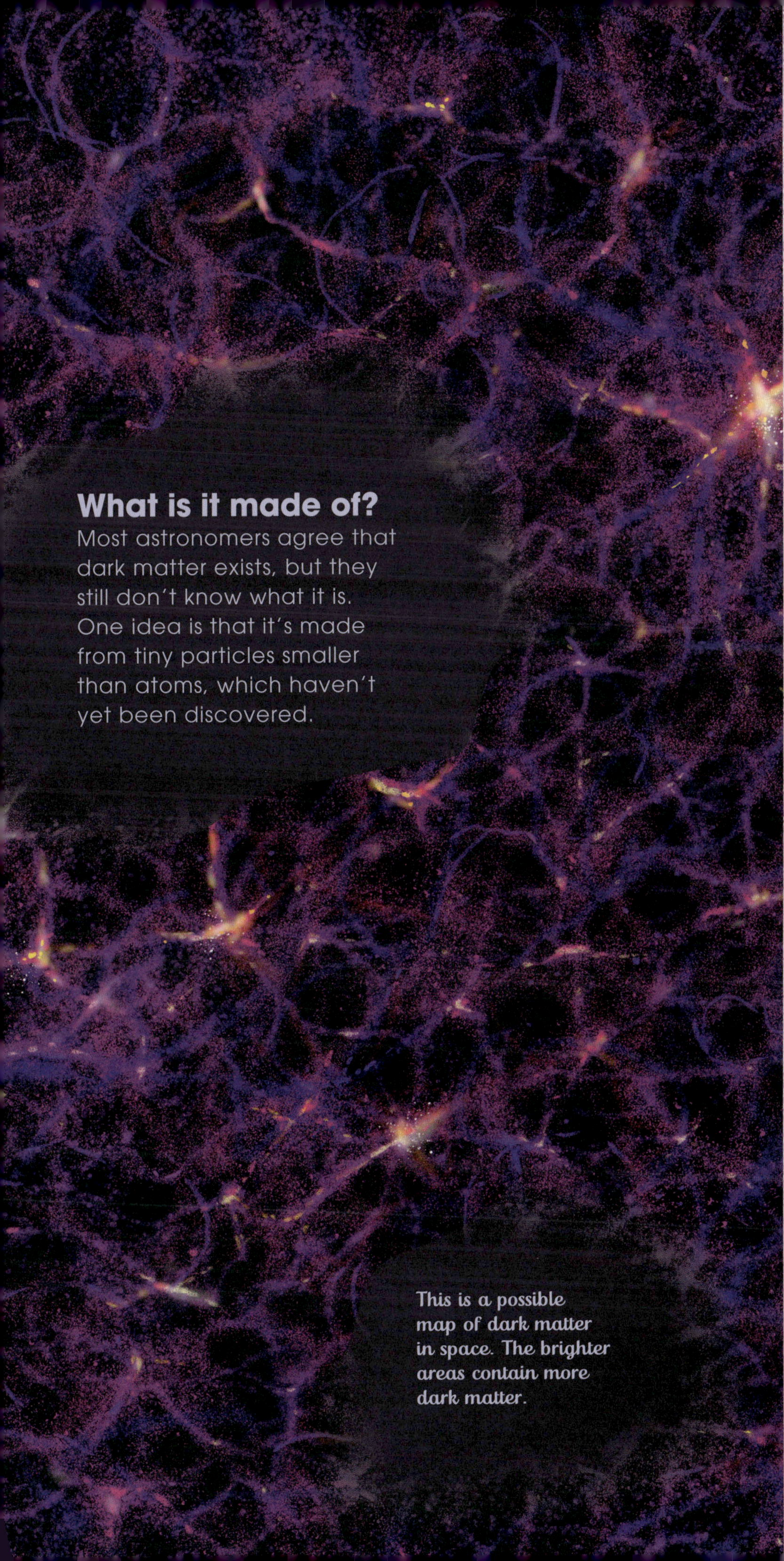

What is it made of?

Most astronomers agree that dark matter exists, but they still don't know what it is. One idea is that it's made from tiny particles smaller than atoms, which haven't yet been discovered.

This is a possible map of dark matter in space. The brighter areas contain more dark matter.

HIDDEN POWER

Dark matter doesn't reflect, absorb, or give off any kind of light, and so it has never been seen directly. Astronomers believe it exists because of how its gravity affects other things in the universe.

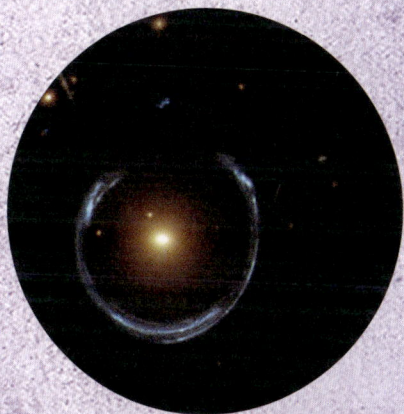

Bending light
Light from distant places can bend around huge objects due to their gravity. We call this gravitational lensing. But the lensing we observe shows that there must be more matter around these objects than we can see.

Searching for answers
Astronomers are working hard to try to understand dark matter better. Planned telescopes, such as the Roman Space Telescope, will help them make brand-new discoveries.

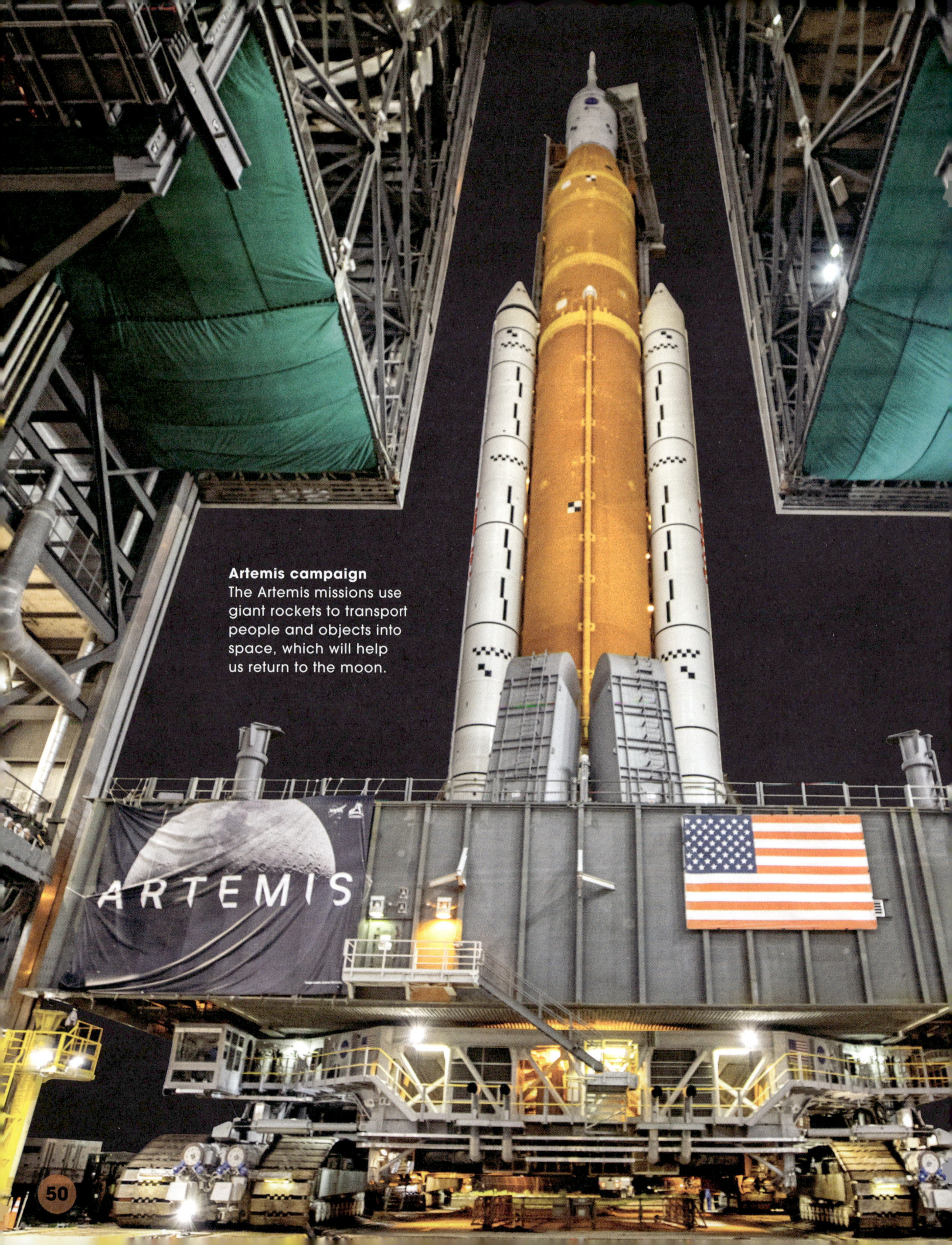

Artemis campaign
The Artemis missions use giant rockets to transport people and objects into space, which will help us return to the moon.

ARTEMIS

EXPLORING SPACE

Humans have been using spacecraft to explore space since the 1950s. Some missions carry astronauts on board, others are robotic and controlled from Earth.

The first spacecraft, Sputnik 1, was a small satellite built by the former Soviet Union, which orbited Earth for three months in 1957. Since then, spacecraft have become bigger and better. They have explored destinations all over our solar system, have helped answer all sorts of questions about space, and have even taken people to the moon.

Walking on the moon

NASA's Apollo program aimed to land astronauts on the moon and return them safely to Earth. It ran from 1961 to 1972, and its high point was in 1969, when the Apollo 11 mission successfully landed astronauts Neil Armstrong and Buzz Aldrin on the surface of the moon.

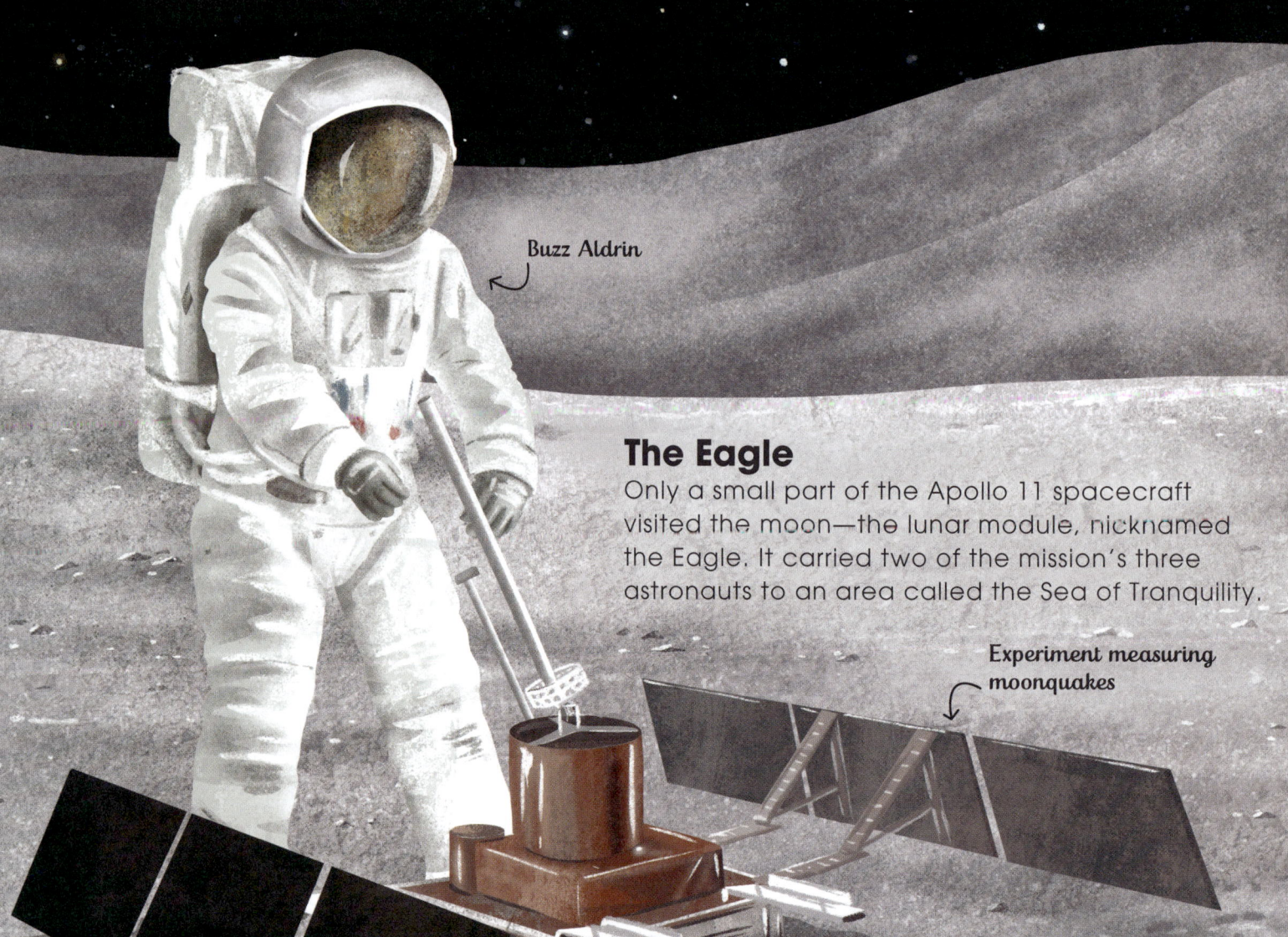

Buzz Aldrin

The Eagle
Only a small part of the Apollo 11 spacecraft visited the moon—the lunar module, nicknamed the Eagle. It carried two of the mission's three astronauts to an area called the Sea of Tranquility.

Experiment measuring moonquakes

Command and service module

Earth

The loneliest man

While Armstrong and Aldrin walked on the moon, a third astronaut, Michael Collins, stayed in another part of the spacecraft—the command module. He was completely alone in lunar orbit for more than 21 hours.

Lunar module

Solar wind experiment

Neil Armstrong

Bootprints

In total, 12 Apollo astronauts walked on the moon during six missions. They launched from Earth on huge Saturn V rockets, which weighed as much as 400 elephants.

Spacecraft entered
Mars' atmosphere

Landing
on Mars

The Perseverance rover
is the size of a small car.
Delivering it safely to Mars'
surface was complex: it
involved a parachute, heat
shield, "sky crane," and
onboard computers.

Parachute
deployed

Heat shield
separated off

Probe checked
the ground below

Space probes

Robotic spacecraft have traveled throughout
our solar system, from the sun and inner planets
all the way out past Pluto. These probes allow
us to explore the solar system and conduct
science in space without sending humans.

Sky crane
containing
the rover
separated
away

Sky crane
powered
the descent

Sky crane
flew away

Rover landed

TOUCHING THE SUN

The Parker Solar Probe orbits the sun very closely. It was the first probe to fly into the corona, to study solar wind.

MERCURY MISSION

MESSENGER was the first probe to orbit Mercury. Its mission improved our understanding of Mercury, and ended in 2015.

VENUS LANDER

Venera 13 survived for 127 minutes on Venus in 1982. This is the longest any lander has survived there.

MOON TWINS

Nicknamed "Ebb" and "Flow," the GRAIL mission's twin spacecraft were used to measure tiny changes in the moon's gravity.

Space probes are built to withstand space conditions—it can be very cold or very hot, and there can be harsh radiation.

IN JUPITER'S ORBIT

Juno has been orbiting Jupiter since 2016. It needs huge solar panels to power it, because it is so far from the sun.

COMET DELIVERY

The Stardust probe collected material from comet 81P/Wild 2, which helped scientists learn about the early solar system.

ASTEROID SAMPLER

The OSIRIS-REx spacecraft made a round trip to asteroid Bennu, to collect precious samples from the asteroid.

FLYING ON TITAN

NASA's Dragonfly probe is a rotorcraft (helicopter) that will explore Saturn's moon Titan, to study if its chemistry could produce life.

The ISS travels around Earth once every 93 minutes. So, it makes 16 orbits every day.

Microgravity science

The ISS allows astronauts to do science experiments in very low gravity. For example, NASA is learning to grow vegetables in space. They have already grown lettuces, tomatoes, and radishes!

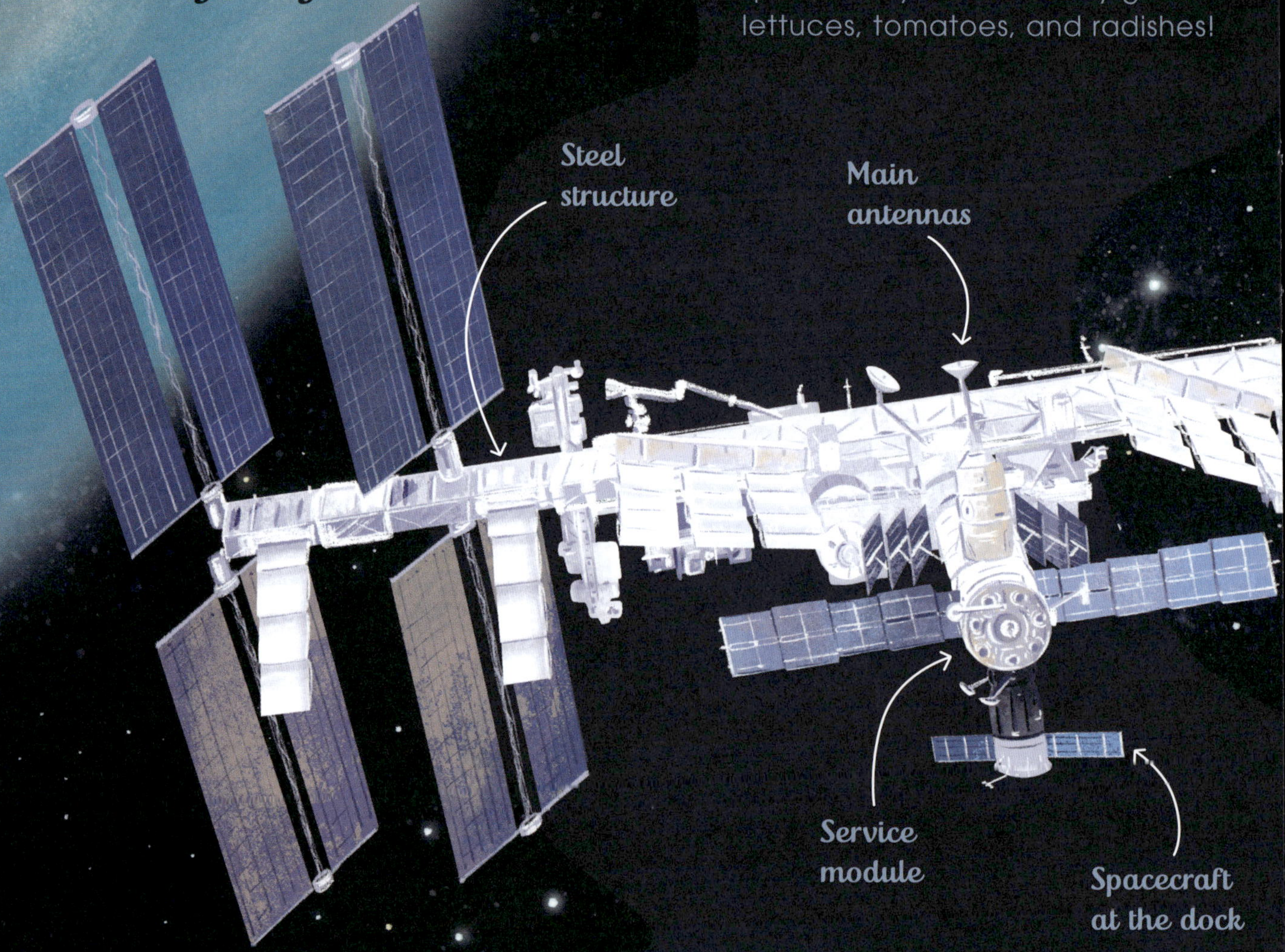

Steel structure

Main antennas

Service module

Spacecraft at the dock

International Space Station

The International Space Station (ISS) is a place where humans can live and carry out experiments in space. The ISS orbits the Earth, staying about 250 miles (400 km) above the surface, and is the largest space station ever built. Five space agencies from around the world work together to maintain the ISS.

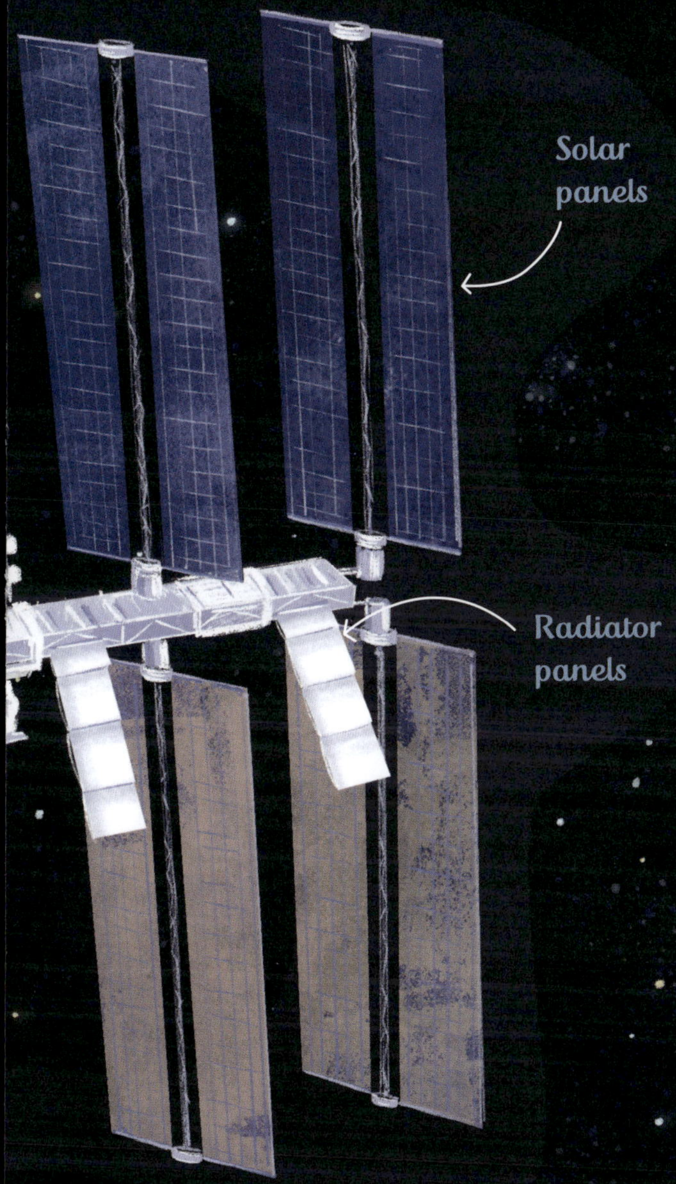

Solar panels

Radiator panels

Living in space
Astronauts have lived on the ISS since 2000. So far, more than 270 people have visited, from more than 20 countries. The record for the longest stay is more than 370 days.

GETTING TO THE ISS
Several different resupply and crew spacecraft have docked with the ISS throughout its history.

SOYUZ
Russian Soyuz spacecraft are one of the main ways of transporting people to the ISS.

SPACE SHUTTLE
NASA's space shuttles flew to the ISS 37 times between 1998 and 2011.

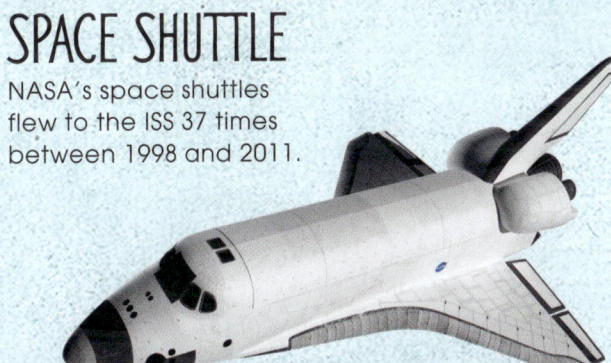

H-II TRANSFER
Japan's H-II Transfer Vehicle is used to send cargo to the ISS.

DRAGON
SpaceX's Dragon spacecraft can carry up to seven people, or cargo, to the ISS.

Animals in space

Animals have been sent into space for decades, to test how living beings can survive on rockets and in places with very low gravity. Many different kinds of animals have made the journey into space, including primates, insects, rodents, frogs, and even tortoises!

Sputnik 2

Tsygan and Dezik

TINY TRAVELERS

Many insects, such as flies and ants, have traveled into space. In 2019, a spacecraft called Beresheet crashed on the moon while carrying a few thousand tiny animals called tardigrades.

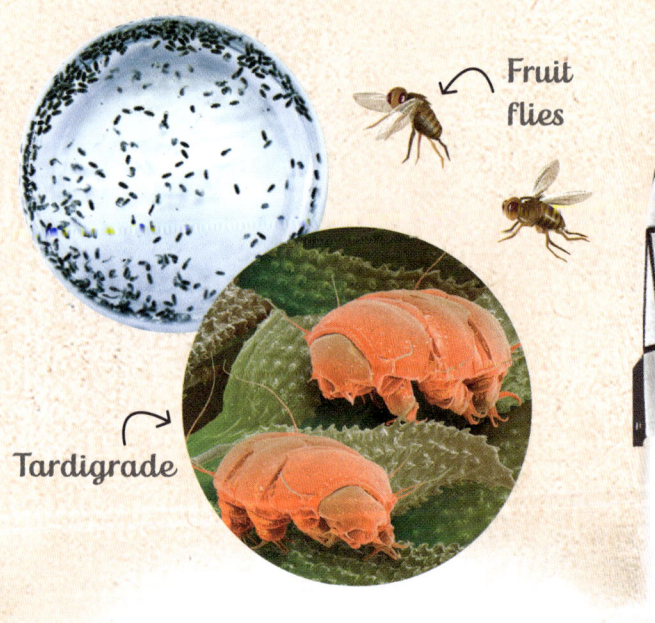

Fruit flies

Tardigrade

The first animals to travel into space were fruit flies, in 1947, to test the effects of radiation on living things at high altitudes.

Laika was the first living thing to orbit Earth, on board Sputnik 2 in 1957.

SPACE DOGS

The former Soviet Union sent several dogs into space in the early days of space exploration. Tsygan and Dezik were the first dogs in space, in 1951.

PRIMATE FLIGHTS

More than 30 monkeys and apes have visited space. Ham, a chimpanzee, made a trip into space on a US rocket in 1961. He was trained to pull levers, and he demonstrated that an animal could perform tasks during spaceflight.

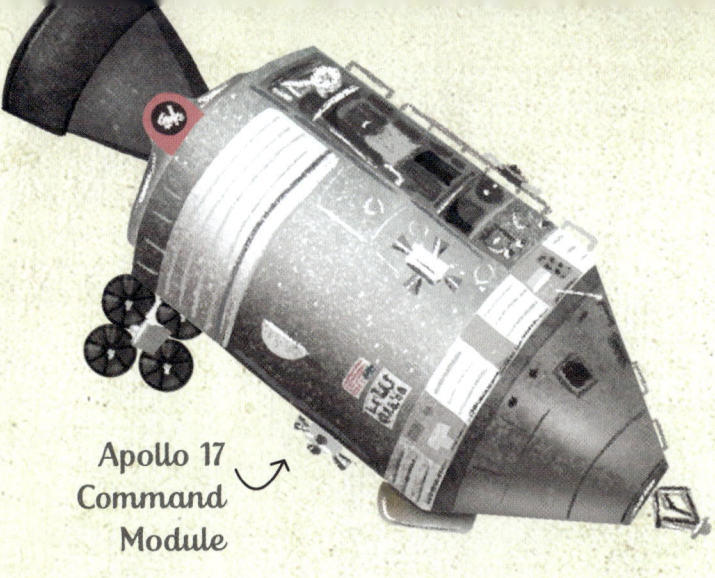

Apollo 17 Command Module

Five mice, Fe, Fi, Fo, Fum, and Phooey, journeyed to lunar orbit on Apollo 17.

Mercury-Redstone 2, Ham's rocket

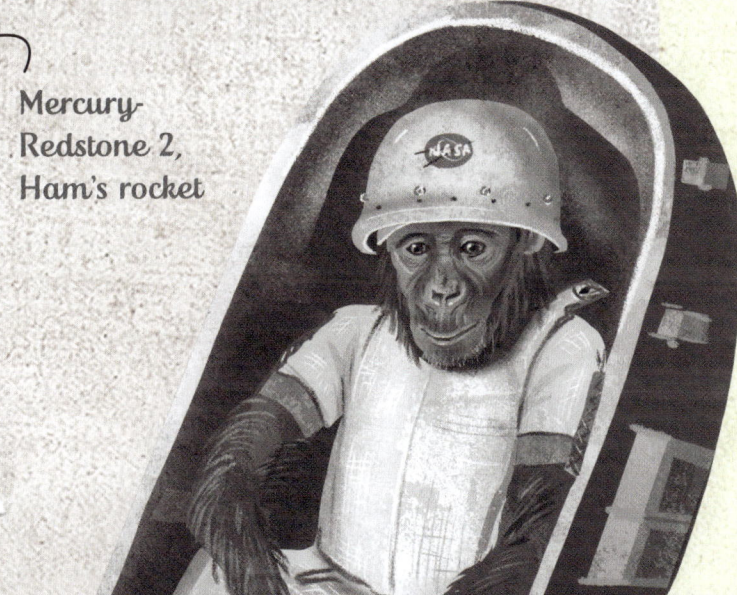

Ham

The first primate in space was Albert II, a rhesus macaque, who reached an altitude of 83 miles (134 km).

This astronaut is conducting experiments on mice on the ISS.

MICROGRAVITY MICE

Many rodents have spent time in space. Mice are often used for biology experiments on the International Space Station, to study how very-low-gravity conditions affect mammals.

There is a network of telescopes around Earth and in space that is dedicated to searching for asteroids that might threaten the planet. They help warn us about likely impacts.

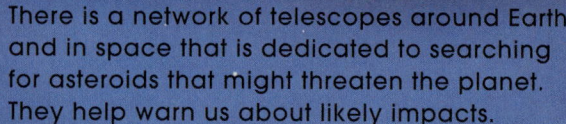
Map of hazardous asteroids

Finding the danger

Near-Earth asteroids are asteroids whose orbits come close to Earth. Those bigger than 460 ft (140 m) across are the most worrying. Scientists believe about 25,000 of these asteroids exist, but we still haven't discovered them all.

DART

Defending Earth

Asteroids often collide with Earth. Small rocks burn up in the atmosphere, but bigger rocks can reach the ground, and a few cause a large amount of damage—such as the event that caused the extinction of the dinosaurs. Taking steps to protect Earth from asteroid impacts is known as planetary defense.

Target practice

Planetary defense experts have suggested several methods for protecting Earth from dangerous asteroids. In one method, something is sent from Earth to hit the asteroid, moving it away from its collision path.

Didymos

Original orbit

New orbit

Dimorphos

The DART mission successfully tested this idea. It hit a small asteroid, Dimorphos, at 4 miles (6 km) per second. The time taken for Dimorphos to orbit around the larger asteroid, Didymos, was shortened by 32 minutes!

The OSIRIS-APEX spacecraft will visit Apophis in 2029.

Apophis

Getting close

Apophis, a near-Earth asteroid about 1,200 ft (370 m) across, is one of the asteroids scientists are most concerned about. When Apophis was discovered, predictions suggested it would hit Earth in 2029. However, we now know it won't hit Earth within the next hundred years.

In April 2029, Apophis will safely pass Earth at a distance of about 20,000 miles (32,000 km). That's about a tenth of the distance between Earth and the moon.

Space junk

Unused, human-made objects that float around in space are known as space junk. The area around Earth is heavily littered with this trash, which can be dangerous. There are about 3,000 dead satellites in orbit, as well as millions of smaller pieces of junk.

The oldest space junk is dead satellite Vanguard 1, which has been

FALLING THROUGH THE SKY

Space junk often falls out of Earth's orbit naturally, and most pieces burn up if they enter Earth's atmosphere. However, sometimes large pieces can reach the ground.

VACUUMING IN SPACE

Several missions have been suggested to help clean up space. Ideas include using a harpoon, a net, or magnets to capture dead satellites and pull them into Earth's atmosphere, where they would burn up.

in orbit since 1958 and is expected to stay there for 240 years.

SPACE CRASHES

Crashes between satellites are rare, but they can happen. In 2009, an operating satellite smashed into a dead one 500 miles (800 km) above Earth, creating thousands of small pieces of space junk.

LOST IN SPACE

Many objects have been dropped and lost by astronauts during their space walks.

Glove
Astronaut Ed White lost a spare glove during the Gemini IV mission in 1965.

Tool bag
A tool bag slipped away from astronaut Heidemarie Stefanyshyn-Piper in 2008, when she was repairing a solar panel on the ISS.

Camera
Astronaut Sunita Williams lost a camera in 2007, when it detached from her.

Destination Mars

No human has left Earth's orbit since the last Apollo mission in 1972, but people have dreamed of traveling to Mars for decades, if not centuries. Space agencies from all over the world are working hard to try and find a way to get astronauts to Mars—and back—safely.

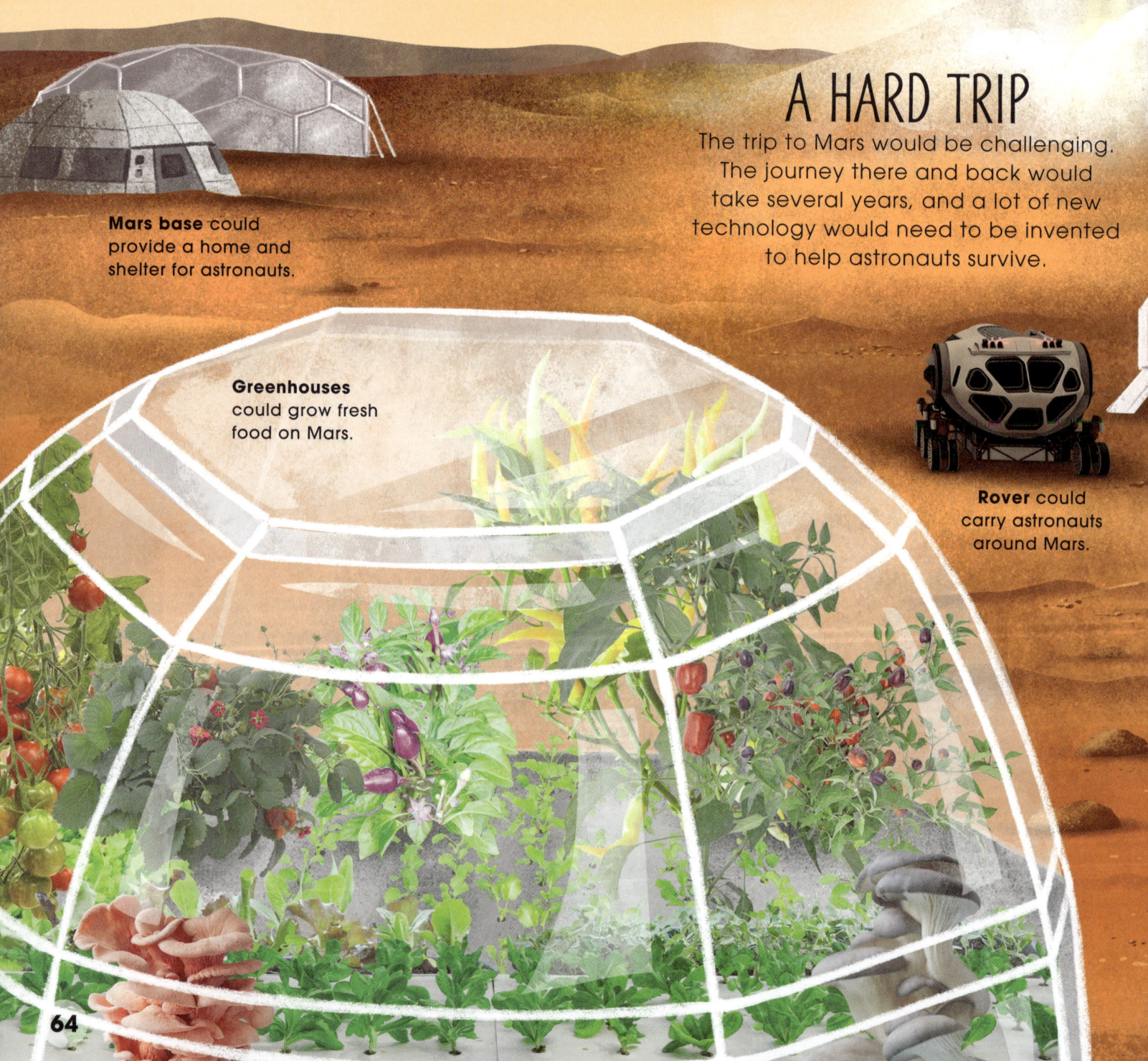

Mars base could provide a home and shelter for astronauts.

A HARD TRIP

The trip to Mars would be challenging. The journey there and back would take several years, and a lot of new technology would need to be invented to help astronauts survive.

Greenhouses could grow fresh food on Mars.

Rover could carry astronauts around Mars.

Powerful rockets could carry astronauts, and would land on Mars as well as lift off from it.

NASA's current Artemis campaign will take people to the moon again. They will learn to live there for long periods, to help NASA prepare for human exploration of Mars.

Communication satellite could send information back to Earth.

Robot explorers such as planes, drones, or helicopters could be used to help astronauts explore.

Labs on Mars could provide a space for astronauts to do fieldwork and science experiments.

Spacesuits could provide air, water, and ways for astronauts to communicate with each other.

MAKING OXYGEN

Oxygen is essential for breathing and fuel. The Perseverance rover did an experiment that proved oxygen can be made from the gases in Mars' atmosphere.

Sun

Mercury

Venus

Earth

Mars

Jupiter

Saturn

Uranus

Neptune

Too hot

Habitable zone

Too cold

Where might aliens live?

So far, Earth is the only place where we know life exists. But ours is just one planet among trillions—surely there must be life out there somewhere? Some scientists dedicate their lives to finding life elsewhere. They search the universe for places where aliens could be.

THE GOLDILOCKS ZONE

We survive on Earth because it is just the right temperature. Any hotter and we would burn; any colder and we would freeze. This just-right distance from the sun is known as the habitable, or "Goldilocks," zone. For another planet to have life, it may need to be in this zone around its star.

LIFE IN WATER

On Earth, all life forms are supported by liquid water. So, the best place to find alien life may be in other places with liquid water. There are a few potential candidates in our own solar system.

Mars

Signs show that water once flowed across the surface of Mars, and that ice is still hidden underground. Life may have been supported by this water millions of years ago.

Mars used to have liquid water.

The Voyager 1 and 2 spacecraft carry sounds and images from Earth, in case they bump into any alien life.

PROFESSIONAL ALIEN HUNTERS

The Search for Extra Terrestrial Intelligence Institute (SETI) is an organization in California, USA, which uses powerful dishes to search for alien life. The dishes receive radio waves from space in the hope they might hear signals from other intelligent beings.

LIFE AS WE DON'T KNOW IT

Astrobiologists (scientists who study the potential for life in space) are focused on looking for Earthlike creatures. But perhaps alien life is so strange to us that we wouldn't even recognize it!

Europa

This moon of Jupiter has a frozen surface, which may hide an ocean of liquid water. There may be life hidden here, similar to the strange life forms that live deep down in Earth's oceans.

Enceladus

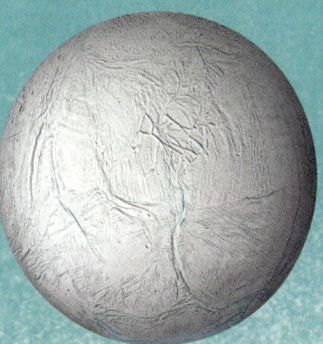

Saturn's moon has icy geysers that shoot up from beneath its frozen surface. The Cassini spacecraft analyzed the jets and showed they contain many of the ingredients for life.

SPACE AND ME

Only a few lucky people will ever get to visit space in person. However, anyone can be a space explorer from here on Earth!

All you have to do to explore space is be curious: ask questions about your place in the universe. People who study space, or build missions that go there, study all kinds of subjects at school. Maybe one day you will find a way to help uncover the mysteries of space!

In the meantime, you can see a little of space yourself, by looking up at the night sky.

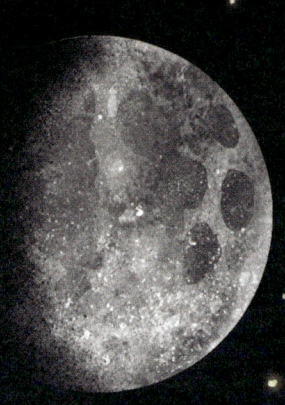

Stargazing

Did you know that you can glimpse the universe from your backyard, or even from your bedroom window? There are even better views away from the bright lights of a town or city. Here are a few ways you can look up and learn for yourself.

Look closer

You can see a surprising amount with just your eyes, such as dark and light patches on the face of the moon. With a pair of binoculars or a telescope, you will be able to see space objects in even more detail—such as Mars' ice cap, Jupiter's moons, and Saturn's rings.

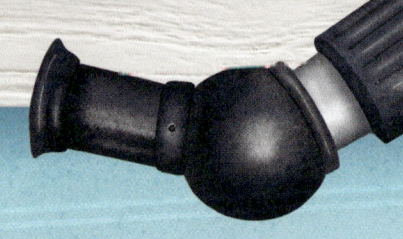

Telescope
Set up a telescope in your backyard for your own personal view of the universe.

Changing moon

You may have noticed that the moon doesn't always look the same. This is because the sun lights different amounts of the moon at different times, depending on where the moon is in its journey around Earth, and where Earth is on its path around the sun. These changes in the moon's appearance are called phases.

New moon
The moon's nearside has no sunlight.

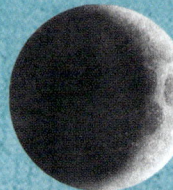

Waxing crescent
A slither of the moon is lit, as seen from Earth.

Centaurus

Ursa major

Orion

Which constellations you will be able to see depends on where you are in the world, and what time of year it is.

Constellations

To help keep track of what's where in the sky, astronomers divide it into sections, called constellations. Each constellation contains a group of stars, which can be joined up to look a little like pictures in the sky.

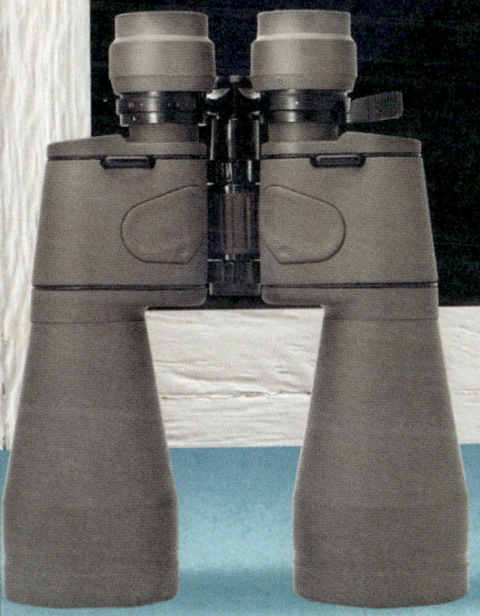

Binoculars
These are easy to use and carry, so you can look at the night sky from anywhere.

Notebook
Keep a record of what you see, to track changes and patterns.

First quarter
Half of the moon's nearside is lit by the sun.

Waxing gibbous
Most of the moon's nearside is in sunlight.

Full moon
The full nearside of the moon is lit.

Waning gibbous
The sunlight on the moon's nearside starts to lessen.

Third quarter
Only one half of the moon's nearside is in sunlight.

Waning crescent
The last slice of the moon's nearside is lit.

Inspired by space

The wonder of space has inspired many artists, writers, and creative thinkers to make great films, books, and paintings. The opposite is also true—many scientists have been inspired to study space because of the marvels shown in stories and art.

Are we alone?

Some of the most popular movies of all time, such as *E.T.* and *War of the Worlds*, look at whether intelligent life might exist off Earth. Would aliens be friendly or hostile?

FROM FICTION TO FACT

Science fiction books and movies explore our relationship with science. They have inspired technology that is now used in space exploration. For example, human space stations and satellite communication were first seen in works of science fiction.

"In praise of mystery"

This poem, by Ada Limón, was inspired by the Europa Clipper mission to Jupiter's moon Europa. The poem has been etched onto the spacecraft, like a message in a bottle.

Astronaut artist

Astronaut Alan Bean became an artist after he returned from the moon. His paintings were inspired by his time on the moon's surface, and contained tiny amounts of moon dust!

Helping Earth

One of the most important things we learn when we explore outer space is that our home—Earth—is precious and worth protecting. Human activity can cause Earth's climate and environment to change. So, we need to work together to protect it and keep it safe for the future.

Collaboration in space

From space, the borders that separate countries are not visible—we are all one Earth. The same is true in space—countries from all over the world work together to explore more of the universe.

Wildfire
smoke

Air quality
Air pollution is tracked by Earth-orbiting
satellites. The data that is collected can
be used to help improve air quality
and human health.

North
America

Pacific
Ocean

Earth monitoring
Many space missions focus
on observing our own planet,
aiming to improve life here
on Earth. They investigate
the oceans, ice, land,
and the atmosphere.

Climate change
Our planet is getting warmer—
particularly the oceans. Earth satellites
help us to track these changes. The red
on this image shows warm water.

South
America

Weather forecasts
Many of the satellites orbiting Earth
are used to make accurate weather
forecasts. These can help us track
major events such as hurricanes,
tornadoes, and forest fires.

Glossary

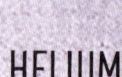

ASTEROID
A small object that orbits the sun, which is usually made of rock, ice, or metal.

ASTEROID BELT
A huge ring, located between the planets Mars and Jupiter, which contains many asteroids.

ATMOSPHERE
The layer of gases that surrounds an object, such as a planet or moon.

ATOM
The basic piece of a chemical element. Atoms are made up of protons, neutrons, and electrons.

BIG BANG
The name given to the event that marked the birth of the universe.

BLACK HOLE
A very dense, ball-shaped region of space, caused by a collapsed star. Light cannot travel fast enough to escape the gravitational pull of a black hole, so it is completely black.

CHEMICAL ELEMENT
A basic substance that makes up all matter. Each chemical element is made from its own type of atom.

COMET
An icy object in the solar system that begins to release gases as it approaches the sun and warms.

CONSTELLATION
A pattern in the sky made by a group of stars. Constellations are often named after mythological figures.

CORE
The innermost layer of a planet, moon, or solid space object. It can be solid or liquid.

CRATER
A bowl-shaped hole in the surface of a planet, moon, or other solid space object. Craters are caused by asteroids, comets, and other smaller space rocks crashing into a surface.

DARK MATTER
Mysterious material that does not absorb, reflect, or emit light.

DENSE
Containing a lot of matter in a small space.

DWARF PLANET
A round object in space that orbits the sun, but that is smaller than a planet. It is not big enough to clear its orbit of other objects.

ECLIPSE
When one object in space moves in front of another and blocks light from reaching an observer.

EXOPLANET
A planet that orbits a star outside our own solar system.

GALAXY
A huge gathering of thousands, millions, or sometimes even billions of stars that swirl together through the universe.

GAS GIANT
A large planet with low density, usually made mainly of hydrogen and helium. In our solar system, Jupiter, Saturn, Uranus, and Neptune are all gas giants.

GRAVITY
The force of attraction that exists between all matter. The larger the mass of an object, the greater its gravitational pull.

HELIUM
The second most common chemical element in the universe, after hydrogen.

HYDROGEN
A chemical element that is found all over the universe. Most stars are mainly made of hydrogen.

KÁRMÁN LINE
The boundary between Earth's atmosphere and space.

KUIPER BELT
A large expanse of the solar system beyond the orbit of the planet Neptune, which contains many small, frozen bodies. Pluto orbits the sun within the Kuiper belt region.

LIGHT YEAR
The distance traveled by light in one Earth year. Light years are used to describe the massive distances between far-away objects in the universe, such as stars and galaxies.

MAGNETIC FIELD
A region around a space body that acts like a shield, protecting it from radiation.

MANTLE
An inner layer of a solid space body that lies between the crust and the core.

METEOR
A small object from outer space that enters Earth's atmosphere, becomes bright, and appears as a streak of light.

METEORITE
A piece of space rock that has made it through Earth's atmosphere to land on the surface of our planet.

METEOROID

A small object moving in the solar system that would become a meteor if it entered Earth's atmosphere.

MILKY WAY

The name of our galaxy.

MOON

The name given to natural objects—big and small—that orbit around various planets in our solar system and beyond.

NEUTRON STAR

The collapsed core of a massive star, left after a supernova.

OORT CLOUD

A huge sphere of icy, comet-like objects that is thought to surround the solar system.

ORBIT

The path an object takes around another—such as the moon's path around Earth.

PARTICLE

A tiny piece of matter.

PLANET

Any one of the eight main worlds in our solar system: Mercury, Venus, Earth, Mars, Jupiter, Saturn, Uranus, and Neptune. There are planets around other stars, too—see "exoplanet."

RINGS

Chunks of material, often icy, that orbit around an object in space.

SATELLITE

Usually refers to the human-made objects that travel around Earth, or other bodies in the solar system. Sometimes, astronomers refer to moons as the natural satellites of planets.

SOLAR SYSTEM

The collection of objects —including planets, moons, asteroids, and comets —that orbit the sun.

SOLAR WIND

Charged particles released by the sun that travel across the solar system.

SOVIET UNION

A huge country that spanned Eastern Europe and Asia from 1922 to 1991.

SPACE JUNK

Human-made debris in space that is no longer in use.

SPACE PROBE

A small, robotic spacecraft.

SPACE STATION

A human-made satellite used as a long-term base for space exploration. The largest space station is the International Space Station.

STAR

An enormous ball of gas that shines brightly.

STARGAZING

Observing stars, often with a telescope.

STAR SYSTEM

A small number of stars that orbit each other, bound by gravity.

SUNSPOT

A dark spot or patch that appears on the sun's surface.

SUN'S CORONA

The gaseous edge of the sun, which is usually visible around the moon during a solar eclipse.

SUPERNOVA

A very powerful explosion created by a large, dying star.

UNIVERSE

All of space and everything it contains.

Index

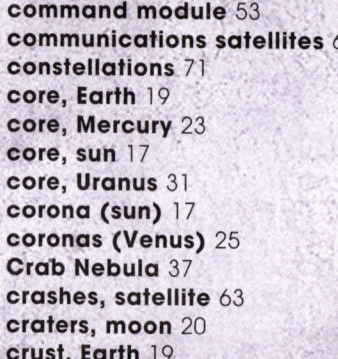

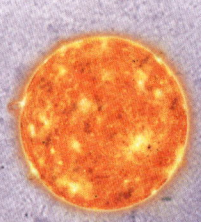

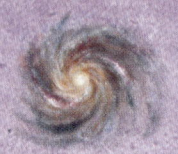
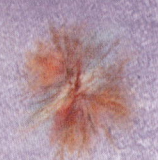

Acknowledgments

The publisher would like to thank the following people for their assistance: Helen Peters for the index, Polly Goodman for proofreading, Sakshi Saluja and Samrajkumar S. for their help with the picture credits.

PICTURE CREDITS

The publisher would like to thank the following for their kind permission to reproduce their photographs: (Key: a-above; b-below/bottom; c-center; f-far; l-left; r-right; t-top)

1-80 Dreamstime.com: Designprintck (Background x29). **4-5 NASA:** NASA Johnson. **6-7 Getty Images:** Carlos Fernandez (ca). **7 NASA:** ESA, CSA, STScI, NIRCam (tc). **8 Alamy Stock Photo:** Helene Rogers / Art Directors & TRIP (tr). **Getty Images / iStock:** luoman (c). **Library of Congress, Washington, D.C.:** F1219 .L56 Copy 2 Provenance; Gift of the Jay I. Kislak Foundation. Includes 3 folded manuscript watercolor drawings of antiquities after illustrations in Clavigero (cl). **9 ESA / Hubble:** W. M. Keck Observatory (cb). **ESO:** F. Marchis, M. Wong, E. Marchetti, P. Amico, S. Tordo (crb). **12-13 Alamy Stock Photo:** Mark Garlick / Science Photo Library. **17 Dreamstime.com:** Daniel Boiteau (crb). **19 NASA:** JPL-Caltech (crb). **21 Dreamstime. com: NASA:** JSC (crb). **Science Photo Library:** NASA / JSC (cb); Detlev Van Ravenswaay (clb); NASA (cb/Goodwill). **24-25 NASA:** JPL (c). **29 Alamy Stock Photo:** Matteo Chinellato (bc); Stephen R. Johnson (crb). **Science Photo Library:** Natural History Museum, London (cb). **33 Dreamstime.com: ESA / Hubble:** MPS (bl). **34-35 NASA:** ESA, CSA, D. Coe (STScI / AURA for ESA; Johns Hopkins University), B. Welch (NASAs Goddard Space Flight Center; University of Maryland, College Park). Image processing: Z. Levay. **37 Dreamstime.com: ESA / Hubble:** NASA, M. Robberto (Space Telescope Science Institute / ESA) and the Hubble Space Telescope Orion Treasury Project Team (clb). **NASA and The Hubble Heritage Team (AURA/STScI):** NASA and The Hubble Heritage Team (STScI / AURA); (crb). **NASA:** ESA, J. Hester and A. Loll (Arizona State University) (cr); JPL-Caltech / Univ.of Ariz (cra). **38 Michael Teoh:** Heng

Ee Observatory, Malaysia (cl); **Shutterstock.com:** PlanilAstro (tl). **39 ESO:** ALMA (NAOJ / NRAO) / E. OGorman / P. Kervella (tr). **Science Photo Library:** John Chumack (c). **45 ESO:** EHT Collaboration, M. Kornmesser, NASA, Lu Amaral (crb). **49 NASA:** ESA / Hubble (cra). **50-51 NASA:** KSC. **52 NASA:** (bl). **53 NASA:** (tr). **57 Alamy Stock Photo:** Sciepro / Science Photo Library (cr); Victor Habbick Visions / Science Photo Library (cra). **NASA:** (clb, cb); Expedition 31 (crb). **58 Science Photo Library:** Look at Sciences / Dung Vo Trung (cl); Babak Tafreshi (cra); Power and Syred (cb); Detlev Van Ravenswaay (crb). **59 Alamy Stock Photo:** NASA Image Collection (tr). **NASA:** (cl, fcl). **60-61 Getty Images:** The Image Bank / Pawel Libera (br). **NASA:** Johns Hopkins University Applied Physics Laboratory. **60 Getty Images:** imageBROKER / Michael Runkel (tr). **63 Alamy Stock Photo:** Planetpix (clb). **Smithsonian National Air and Space Museum:** Photo by Dane Penland / NASM2014-05409 (cra). **64 Dreamstime. com:** Just_Regress (b); Zygotehasnobrain (cb). **NASA:** (cr). **65 NASA:** (br); JPL (tr); JPL-Caltech (cr). **66 Dreamstime.com:** Archangel80889 (bc). **67 Dreamstime. com:** Planetfelicity (clb). **NASA:** JPL-Caltech (bc). **68-69 Dreamstime.com:** Ginettigino. **71 Dreamstime.com:** Arsgera (cl). **72 Alamy Stock Photo:** Chroma Collection (bl). **73 NASA:** (tr, crb); JPL-Caltech (tc). **74-75 NASA. 75 Alamy Stock Photo:** Phil Degginger (cb); Stockimo / Adam Welz (c); Geopix (f). **NASA:** (b).

Cover images: Front: Alamy Stock Photo: Walter Myers / Stocktrek Images fcla, Martin cla; **Depositphotos Inc:** studio-fi tr; **Dreamstime.com:** Nerthuz cla/ (Rocket), Solarseven cr; **Getty Images:** Ian McKinnell ftr, SCIEPRO cb; **NASA:** Reto Stöckli, based on data from NASA and NOAA clb; Back: **Alamy Stock Photo:** Martin tc; **Depositphotos Inc:** studio-fi bc; **Dreamstime.com:** Nerthuz clb, Solarseven cra; **Getty Images:** Ian McKinnell cb; **NASA:** Reto Stöckli, based on data from NASA and NOAA tr; Spine: **Dreamstime. com:** Solarseven cb; **NASA:** Reto Stöckli, based on data from NASA and NOAA bc/ (Globe).

All other images © Dorling Kindersley

ABOUT THE AUTHOR

Shoshana Z. Weider is a planetary scientist and writer. She is originally from London, but now lives in Washington DC, where she works at NASA Headquarters in the Planetary Science Division. She gets to work with many of the teams who build and run some of the missions featured in this book. She has already written one book, *Moon Landings*, for DK and is working on another. Shoshana loves to talk to kids about the wonders of space and inspire the next generation of explorers.

ABOUT THE ILLUSTRATOR

Claire McElfatrick is a freelance artist. Her beautiful hand-drawn and collaged illustrations are inspired by her home in rural England. Claire has illustrated all the other books in this series: *The Magic and Mystery of Trees, The Book of Brilliant Bugs, Earth's Incredible Oceans, The Extraordinary World of Birds, The Frozen Worlds,* and *Prehistoric Worlds.*